The Worlds End
Chelsea unplugged

Peter D Painter

© 2012 by Peter Devenport
All rights reserved. Copyright under Berne Copyright Convention, Universal Copyright Convention, and Pan-American Copyright Convention. No part of this book may be reproduced, stored in a retrieval system, or transmitted in any form, or by any means, electronic, mechanical, photocopying, recording or otherwise, without prior permission of the author

ISBN 978-1-291-33998-7

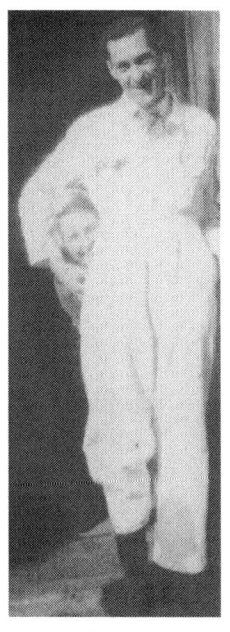

For my loving parents Joyce and Cyril.

I would like to thank all of the characters that made up life as it was in the good old Worlds End, especially the girls, my sisters, Pauline, Carol, Sue and Karen who have been so supportive and sharing with their memories. To all of my friends for their encouragement, which has meant so much, and thanks must go especially to Janet Bord for her much valued literary expertise. And last but not least special thanks must go to my partner Judy Young who has been so patient, and has helped me with her much valued input and her tireless dedication, but above all her belief in this book.

Contents

Acknowledgements

Introduction *4*

1. Worlds End and family beginnings *8*

2. Dead end street *20*

3. The reformed monarchist *38*

4. Oh! I do like to be beside the seaside *43*

5. We are the Chelsea boys *54*

6. The best room *73*

7. The wonderful Mrs G *79*

8. The first streaker *89*

Photographs *98*

9. Get out of that *115*

10. Hospital job *122*

11. Bleak house *127*

12. The exorcist *133*

13. Famous faces, famous places *144*

14. Right on the nose *159*

15. Nice one Cyril *164*

INTRODUCTION

Chelsea is a place that most people today associate with Hooray Henrys and Sloane Rangers cruising around their hoity-toity world in their Chelsea tractors. Dolly-birds and the Kings Road may also come to mind; and then there is the football club along with its Russian oligarchs with their massive yachts and equally massive egos; but above all there is that other Chelsea requisite - loads of money. There was once, however, a very different Chelsea, which showed another side to this magnetic place. This was the Chelsea of my grandparents, my parents and my own - a Chelsea of extended families, many shops and many factories, a Chelsea where the working class was King and their capital was a small collection of streets called the Worlds End ... and at the heart of these stories is my father, Cyril.

His Chelsea, or the Worlds End, spread out around the old traffic-island which once existed on that busy artery, the Kings Road. The traffic island was surrounded on all sides by a great variety of shops, many of which were family-owned, with up to three generations working in them at any one time: there was a fish and chip shop, where the proprietor, just as in the two butchers' shops and the dairy, wore a white work-coat. A choice of fruit and veg. was available from the brown-coated sellers, at either the green grocers shop or the two barrows - one at the top of our street or the other which was rolled out and set up daily outside the old Salvation Army Hall. There was the Home and Colonial store which sold just about everything to do with food. This was replaced in the 1960s by one of the first hippy shops in London, Gandalfs Garden. There was a haberdashery, inside which was found all the necessities for home-made clothing, from thread and needles to the great variety of wools so common-place amongst the ladies, who all knitted constantly for their ever-growing broods; and right next door to this was a lady's clothes shop. Another most valuable shop was the hardware store, or the oil shop, as it was known, where you were served by a Mr

Goodrich, who always wore a green work-coat; there you could buy just about anything practical, from string and panes of glass to paraffin (the paraffin would give it the name by which it was known). There was also that staple ingredient of old London, once so familiar to us all - the junk shop.

The Kings Road runs a short distance away, and parallel to, the Thames, and just like this great old river, runs daily back and forth with its ever-changing flow of human tides and currents. As it passed through the old Worlds End a great whirlpool of energy was created as it swirled around the old traffic-island at its heart. Whirlpools can be dangerous, but they can also be exciting, and such was the case with this particular one, for it was this swirling energy that, I believe, gave the old Worlds End so much of the character that marked it out from the rest of West London, attracting the great diversity of people that made up the close community of Worlds Enders.

Unfortunately for us, nearly all of the old Worlds End along with many of its colourful residents would be swept away in the developing madness that affected so much of Britain in the late 1960s. The demolition men would move in to erase not only the traffic-island but all the surrounding buildings, including St. Johns Church, the Salvation Army Hall, and the many shops and most of the streets which made up this once vibrant and interesting community.

Our street, Slaidburn Street, was thankfully to survive the destruction of the developers, and would be left as almost the last fragment of the real Worlds End, allowing my father Cyril to end his days where he had begun them. Cyril was a tremendous character, and like all characters was, throughout his life, to attract many interesting people into his world; there was never a dull moment, and I was most fortunate to be able to spend so much time with him, and witness his unique character at work and at play.

He was also a great teacher, and throughout his life he would teach me many things, two of which have been invaluable on my own journey. First, was to always be yourself, and throughout his life this was something that he never compromised, whether in the presence of the Queen, or just down at the pub with his, or, as was often the case, my mates. Second was to do with punctuality: this was something that he always managed, even with the busy schedule of a London builder, and one day when I caused him to be late for an appointment he gave me this wonderful piece of advice, 'You can do what you like with your own time, but never waste the time of other people. It's not yours to waste.' His life was a great example of generosity, kindness, humour, and more importantly, honesty, for even if you didn't like what he had to say at least you could be sure that he was telling the truth; this is a gift in itself, and something that was treasured by all of his many friends.

I hope this will all become clear as you read about him and the various incidents that happened to and around him, and my hope is that in some way I have managed to convey the many good qualities of an ordinary man who, with so much against him at the beginning of his life, not only managed to make it such a great success, but along the way would also enrich the lives of all who were fortunate enough to have known him.

One thing is certain, the world would be a far better place if there were more people like Cyril, for it is certainly a far poorer place without him.

CHAPTER ONE

WORLDS END AND FAMILY BEGINNINGS

I would rather start a family than finish one
-Don Marquis.

In the beginning there was the end, the Worlds End. Well, there was for me, as the Worlds End, Chelsea, was the place where I, like my father Cyril and his parents before him happened to be born; and as if being born in the Worlds End was not enough of a challenge, our beginnings would also be in a cul-de sac, or as we called it, 'a dead-end street'. For myself, I find it hard to imagine a better place to have been born, but being the 1950s it was a whole different world to the one that my grandparents knew, where the words 'dead-end' and 'worlds end' were far more literal.

Charles Booth, the historian, social reformer and founder of the Salvation Army, in his 1899 survey of living conditions in London described Slaidburn Street thus: 'A cul-de-sac, asphalt paved one of the worst streets in Chelsea and I should say one of the worst in London, drunken, rowdy, constant trouble to police: many broken patched windows, open doors, drink-sodden women at windows.'

Slaidburn Street would fall at the bottom of Booth's seven-colour-coded map, earning the classification of 'black', which he termed as 'vicious and semi-criminal', adding in his notes: 'The lowest class, which consists of some occasional labourers, street sellers, loafers, criminals and semi-criminals. Their life is the life of savages, with vicissitudes of extreme hardship and their only luxury is drink.' This was a pretty good description of the Worlds End if ever there was one.

So, this was the world that Cyril's parents, my grandparents, began their lives. Cyril's father, William Devenport, was born in 1884, and his mother, Ellen, in 1886. They were married in 1905 and would go on to have seven children. William Devenport, being the son of an Irish horse dealer (or 'stealer', as Cyril would joke) was a farrier by trade and worked in a blacksmith's yard in the now very fashionable

Glebe Place, just a short way along the Kings Road from the Worlds End.

He began his working life at thirteen, which was common for the time, and his trade, being so hard and physical, would make him into a very strong man indeed: this would be something he would use to earn much-needed extra cash. Street-gambling played a big part in the lives of many people back then, even though it was illegal, but this, as is so often the case, would make it even more alluring. Bets would be placed on just about anything, and so it is no surprise that his strength would be put to the test in some very novel ways. One such way would involve an upright piano which would be carried by several men from the pub into the street, a chalk line would then be drawn on the cobbles some way down the road and bets were then placed upon his ability to carry the piano, which was now strapped to his back, down the road and across the line. The second, even more incredible feat of strength, involved him lifting a horse onto his back. He would crawl underneath, and bets were placed on his being able to clear all four feet of the horse from the ground. This dangerous bet he carried out many times, and I'm sure it made him some much-needed money.

With the outbreak of World War One his skill as a farrier was required to maintain some of the many horses used by all the armed services during this bloody and mindless conflict, and like many of the young men in France at this time, he would, sadly, be exposed to the gas used by the Germans which would leave lasting damage to his lungs.

His war came to an end when he got into a fist-fight with another soldier, who fell hitting his head on a gun-carriage. The soldier died from his head wound, and as a consequence William was court-marshalled, dishonourably discharged from the forces, and returned home, like many others a broken man. This big, likeable, tough guy never recovered from these experiences and died in 1931 at the age of forty seven leaving Cyril, now aged eight, along with his six brothers and sisters, to face a difficult and uncertain future without their father. Cyril's mother would now have the unenviable task of facing life without her husband, to which would be added the further cruel burden (even after many written appeals) of no means of support from the state, including no war pension, with which to help her family.

Cyril's mother Ellen, or Nell, as she was more commonly known, was the product of a by no means uncommon liaison between her mother, who was in service as a maid, and the philandering aristocrat who was her employer. The identity of her father still remains a family mystery, although my grandmother always maintained that she was a 'Lady' by right, although not by title. Strangely, a title did come into the family through the marriage of her granddaughter, also named Ellen, to the actor Sir Stanley Baker. As they say, 'What comes around goes around.'

Ellen was brought up in a small cottage at the bottom of the Worlds End Passage by someone she always referred to as her 'Gran'. This lady was to act as her surrogate mother, and would also be her teacher, supplying her with a rudimentary education which we can only assume had been financed by her father. When she was eight years old her father sent a horse-drawn carriage to collect her. Obviously, in a fit of conscience he had decided to take her in, but what he hadn't reckoned for was the reaction he would get to this plan. She was taken to what she described as 'a huge house', which upon entering so upset her that she immediately went into a rage, followed by many tears. Being inconsolable and even uncontrollable, her father, whatever had been his intentions, would have no alternative but to return her to the lady she had always called Gran, and to the more intimate and familiar surroundings that were more to her liking.

Her ability to read and write would be something that would serve her well in later years and would enable her to act as an unpaid secretary for her mostly illiterate neighbours. She would also carry out another important function for this tight community, making out the 'Sheet', as it was known. This was a collection to buy flowers from all the neighbours upon the passing of one of their own. Upon the Sheet they would scribble their names and the amount of their contribution. Strangely, these same functions would fall to my own mother, who many times - even as late as the 1970s - would sit down with one of her neighbours to read to them (as some were still illiterate) any written correspondence which they happened to receive, and she would also carry on the street tradition of making up the Sheet.

The other important function that Gran always carried out upon a death in the street was the laying-out of the body. She would first carefully close the eyes and mouth, then gently wash their body, chatting away to them very matter-of-factly, saying things like, 'We can't have you going out looking like that now, can we. What would people think?' She would dress them, do their hair, and finally, lovingly lay them out, 'Now presentable,' as she put it, to await the undertaker who would take them away to prepare them for the funeral. Gran was equally adept at the beginning of life and would act, again like my mother, as midwife to many of her family, friends and neighbours - for most people, including myself and all of my sisters, were born at home. Communities really did look after each other.

Having repeatedly been refused any support from all the authorities, Ellen had no choice but to find work in order to support her fatherless brood. This she did by doing general laundry at the dreaded Chelsea work-house in Sydney Street, which was a place of last resort for the poorest of the poor.

Some of Cyril's earliest memories come from this time, for having lost his father this young lad would throw in his lot to help with all the family chores, and even though he was merely eight years old he nevertheless seemed to relish the responsibility, and was an invaluable help not only to his mother but to the rest of the family. He would help with the many chores of running the home, even beginning the evening meal which he had prepared with his mum, before he went off to school and she had set off for her long day's work. She would return home to find fires lit and dinner under way.

It was to be these family chores that, I believe, were to form so much of his character, and in particular his unique cooking abilities. Cyril in the kitchen was always a sight to behold; his one and only way to make a meal was to put as much into it as he could lay his hands on, which was something that could have only come from his early years when there were so few ingredients available. It must be said that his soups, and especially his bangers and mash, were a real treat.

Another of his early memories revolved around the unpleasantness that was the once-weekly bath night. This weekly ritual would take place in the scullery, which was a tiny room which combined kitchen, wash-room and bathroom. A large vessel, known as a copper, was filled with hot water from kettles to which was added washing soda, a strong lime-based powder, in which his mother first did the washing. The washing done, bath-time could begin in the very same water. His father would always be first, followed by the rest of the family, one by one in order of age. They were each given a thorough scrubbing with a bristle brush, and on leaving the water were dried with coarse towels, leaving their skin red and sore.

This ritual left quite a mark on Cyril, who throughout the rest of his life considered one bath a week, always on a Sunday, more than adequate; indeed to bath any more than once a week carried a threat, or as he would put it, 'You'll wash yourself away' - something he would always repeat to both myself and my sisters

At age sixteen Cyril was to meet my mother Joyce, whose own childhood journey had not exactly been a bed of roses.

She was born in 1924 on a farm in a small Essex village. Her memories of this time were few, as she was to lose her mother at the tender age of four. Nevertheless, she could still remember riding on a horse-drawn farm cart, and would tell us of her bedroom with its thatch-covered dormer-window. Upon the death of her mother, her father through necessity remarried, in order to replace the mother of his three children, taking them from the farm to live in Carshalton on the opposite edge of South London. Unfortunately for them, they now fell under the control of the archetypal wicked step-mother, a woman called Lizzie Maud, who was small and extremely cruel - so much so, that in order to escape her cruelty my mother would run away consistently.

Eventually, at the age of thirteen, she would escape for good, going to live with her aunt at her home in Fulham. From there she was soon to find her way to her other aunt and uncle, who just happened to live in Slaidburn Street, which was, of course, the home of Cyril. They soon began courting and were to marry in 1941, Cyril being eighteen, and Joyce, my mother, a mere seventeen.

Auntie Emma and Uncle Frank lived in number 15 Slaidburn

Street, and Cyril with his family, in number 13. Upon their marriage my parent's first and only home was to be at number 17, so Cyril was born in 13, married the girl from 15, and went to live in 17 - all very odd.

My mother's first action as the new Mrs Devenport was to rescue her two brothers from the clutches of the wicked step-mother. Off she went to Carshalton, to return with my uncles Bill and Jim, who would move into number seventeen, creating a ready-made family for Joyce and Cyril. It says so much about both of them, that their first action as a newly married couple was to help others ... this was something they were to continue to do for the rest of their lives.

These were of course the war years and Cyril like most young men was keen to do his bit. He tried to enlist in the RAF, but during the required medical examination was found to be suffering from TB which much to his annoyance meant that he was refused admittance, and as a consequence was immediately packed off to a sanatorium for treatment. Cyril was never one to be idle, and after many escapes back to his young bride in Chelsea, Joyce, seeing how miserable he was, decided that she would treat him herself - and this she did with great success. Part of her treatment was the invention of something she always called her Jollopp, which was a mixture of herbs and honey, and along with her natural ability as a healer Cyril was to gradually reclaim some of the considerable amount of lost weight and was soon able to resume a normal life. Cyril was to use Jollop for the rest of his life, and a very successful cure-all it always turned out to be.

Although being denied the chance to actually go to war Cyril would certainly play his part at home, as London was to experience the horrors of the Blitz which touched upon the lives of all Londoners. Just like so many others he rarely talked about the war, but there was to be one exception to this as it had shaken him so badly that he just had to let it out.

On the night of the 23rd of February 1944 one of the four blocks of the Guinness Trust estate which was just a couple of hundred yards from Slaidburn Street was hit during a heavy raid. Most of the residents had taken shelter in the basements of the five-storey buildings, but unfortunately many of those in the block that was hit were to be trapped there. The rescue services, aided by many of the locals including Cyril, fought desperately to free them from the mountains of rubble, and many were saved. Unfortunately, however, eighty six people were to lose their lives that night, most being brought out of the basement which had by this time flooded. This had left Cyril with the awful memory of seeing them, many of whom were women and children, brought out quite dead, but without a scratch.

It's difficult to imagine what those dark years did to so many peoples' lives so it will come as no surprise that the inhabitants of Slaidburn Street, just like many other Londoners, would now have themselves one hell of a party to celebrate VE (victory in Europe) day which would soon be followed by VJ (victory over Japan) day.

Being a cul-de-sac Slaidburn street was perfect for these large parties, and in no time at all the street would be decorated with flags and bunting; trestle tables were placed along the centre of the road and all the children were sat down to enjoy a communal feast which had all been made by the many housewives of the street. With bellies now full they would then be entertained by various street-performers which included Punch and Judy shows and even black and white minstrels. Meanwhile the adults would be enjoying themselves with a few well-earned beers brought in by the wooden crate full of quart-size bottles from the conveniently placed Watneys beer factory just around the corner. Street parties would continue to happen in Slaidburn Street most notably for the coronation of Her Majesty the Queen in 1952, for which Cyril and Joyce organised a collection for the purchase of bone-china memorial cups and saucers which were given to all the children. The Street's last party would be in 1977 to celebrate the same Queens Silver Jubilee for which as a sign of the changing times our new neighbour, the actress Nyree Dawn Porter, encouraged by her fellow Thespians the glorious Joan Greenwood and husband Andre Morell, was seen upon a step ladder dressed in a skirt and bikini top painting a large mural across the wall at the far end declaring 'God Save The Queen'.

With the war now over life could begin to return to a kind of normality, and Cyril would set out on his journey as a working man.

Cyril began his working life firstly as a 'shiner' or window-cleaner, but he was soon to find his real talent as a painter and decorator. Employment at this time was mainly provided by one of the many factories peppering the great River Thames. There was Prices Candle Factory across the river in Battersea which, when the wind blew from the South, would permeate all the streets of the Worlds End with its strange aroma of boiled animal hooves which were used in the manufacture of their products. There were two bottling-plants, one for Watneys beer, which was one of the largest employers in the area, and the other was Brown and Pank, who dealt mostly in spirits, sherries and wines. There were also the many small family-owned businesses such as butchers, bakers and dairies, who would employ many of the young lads, initially as delivery boys, who would roam the streets on trade-bikes with their square iron-frame at the front, into which fitted a large wicker basket to carry their deliveries. If any of the boys showed initiative they were then taught the tricks of the chosen trade. The local factories would announce lunch-breaks and the end of the working-day with loud sirens, these would shortly be followed by the crunching of wooden clogs as all the workers made their way home along the Kings Road. This would continue into the 1960s.

Obviously none of these jobs appealed to the young Cyril who, it seems, had already made up his mind to forge his own path. Starting on his own, he was soon to be seen pushing his hand-cart, loaded with ladders and materials, all over Kensington and Chelsea, and many years later whilst driving around the area with him, he would point out many of the jobs with which he had started his career. One in particular I still look upon with a kind of horror. This is a flag-pole on top of a large mansion block at the back of Kensington High Street. Cyril, working alone, had attached his ladder to the pole in order to paint it - a formidable task even today - and to do it alone ... well!

With his great character and being such a good worker his reputation began to spread, and through increasing demand for his skills he was soon able to employ his first workmen. His big breakthrough would be to meet his first lady interior decorator, a Mrs Vickers, who was then to introduce him to his long-time friend and most valuable provider of work, the wonderful Mrs G, of whom there shall be more later.

At the time of my entry into Cyril's world (1955) he had, by sheer hard work and full use of his enormous character, built up his business, employing at its peak over thirty workmen of all trades. By 1963 he was able to purchase his, and the Street's, first new car. This was an enormous achievement, as cars at this time were few - in fact, there were only two others in Slaidburn Street, neither of which were new. This was soon followed by the purchase of a brand new Bedford van, proudly bearing his company name, *C. Devenport, Ltd.*

With Cyril now on a roll he would also brush shoulders with the shady world of politics, and this began with his standing for chairman of the local Conservative club. The club up until the mid-sixties was deemed a bit stuffy for most of the working class locals, but with Cyril's election victory it would over time become a popular place for all and sundry. At the time of his election in1965 Cyril, at forty-two, would be the youngest man to hold this position in the club's history, and he was to continue as chairman until 1983, throughout this time making the once quiet club into a busy and profitable one. He would also be active in many aspects of local politics, and the Tory party, recognising a good thing when they saw it (Cyril being a popular man as well as a good communicator) groomed him for bigger roles within their hallowed ranks. Unfortunately, being an honest man, something that is sorely missing in the political world, he would soon be filtered out of their system, as he on various occasions refused to toe the line, or to put it more bluntly, he would not vote against his conscience, for he always considered that doing what was right was far more important than doing what you're told. Around the same time he would also become a Freemason; this, just as with his other role at the club, involved him in many meetings requiring a lot of socialising, which of course meant a lot of drinking, and was really just another way of having a good night out with the boys.

These were some of his best days, and as my older sisters have told me, were the happiest times for the whole family. There were endless parties on Saturday nights, where family and friends would all gather in our best room to have a good old knees-up. A number of chairs were placed along the walls of the room especially for the old folk, including Gran. There they would sit watching all the fun going on around them, whilst constantly being topped up with their favourite drink, which was either Mackeson or Guinness: these were dark stouts, that were almost obligatory for the older generation, who believed it was good for the blood. For the rest there were stacks of wooden crates, filled with quart-size bottles of beer, all sorts of spirits, and the very fashionable small bottles of Babycham, which were a favourite of the ladies, and were also given in small amounts to most of us kids.

Being a party, of course we had to have music. In those days most people were capable of doing a turn, and Cyril himself was a dab-hand on his old Hohner piano-accordion; and then there would be a great collection of 78 records which we played on our wonderful old HMV radiogram with its fascinating hydraulic lid, which when released would close slowly and very gently. The records we played were quite a mixture, being a strange collection of piano songs by Winifred Atwell, the occasional Pat Boone song (he being a heart-throb of my sister Pauline), and lots of Elvis; but my favourites by far were the fabulous collection of imported 78s of the outrageous Little Richard which were brought to the party by our neighbour, Billie Lowe.

As the party wound down and all the records had been played, it would always end with Gran being serenaded by one of Cyril's best friends, Tommy Casey. Tommy, being Irish, like most of his kin could belt out a good song, and Gran would sit looking up at him as he closed the night with the inevitable 'Danny Boy' followed by her old favourite, 'Nellie Dean', changing it as usual to Nellie D. It never failed to bring a tear to her eyes.

Unlike the majority of the older people in the Street who lived quite sensibly on the ground floor, Gran was to see out her days up in her two familiar top-floor rooms: a bed-sitting room which looked down upon the street and a small kitchen at the back. The bed-sitting room was filled with all the bits and bobs of her long life. There was a dresser against one wall with a collection of china, some photographs and many other nick-nacks, a chest of drawers between the two windows, upon which stood her large black and white television, and last but not least her big brass bed, in which she would lie to receive her visitors. Although later in her life she would hardly leave her two rooms, this seemed to have little effect upon her knowledge of all the things going on around her, for she was, as we used to say, 'Psychic as a bat'. She never ceased to amaze us with her insight.

Just like Cyril, she was also totally honest with her comments and observations, although sometimes these would lack more than a little tact. One day a relative of ours came to show off her new baby, and several of us accompanied her to visit Gran. The baby was handed to Gran in her bed. She kissed the baby, and then casually announced to the room full of people, 'Ah she's lovely, but she's not long for this world'. A stunned silence fell on the room, but was quickly passed over as we all pretended that we had not heard her grave prediction. Gran was usually right with her predictions, and unfortunately this was to be the case with the fate of the baby which, just as she'd prophesied, would pass away a mere two weeks later.

Visiting her upon our birthdays was a family ritual and always guaranteed to be fun. As usual, there she would be propped up in her big brass bed, smiling away as she always did, and after a kiss and of course a 'Happy birthday', she would ask us to leave the room for a couple of minutes. From the landing outside we would stand silently, listening as Gran went through her little ritual. We would hear the squeak as she unscrewed one of the brass knobs from the top of her bed. This was followed by a little rustling, and then more squeaks as she replaced the knob. 'You can come back in now', she would announce, and in we would go, the lucky birthday girl or boy would then be presented with a ten bob note, from her not so secret hiding place. She was lovely, she never complained and always had a smile on her pretty face. Just like Cyril, she was of a positive and happy nature. What a great example she set to us all.

She died in 1972 at the good age of eighty-six, and after a brief spell with the undertakers, she was brought back to the Street where she had spent her life, to lie in state proper in our best room at number 17. This was the custom at the time and one that gave a great intimacy to the precious last few days that we could share with her. It would be the first time that I would experience this very personal way of paying tribute to a loved one, but alas, it would not be the last.

The best-room was on the first floor and would be carefully prepared for her final return to the Street: white sheets were hung over the two windows, one window being left slightly open, so it was said: 'to allow her soul to leave'. A cross, candlesticks and incense burners were borrowed from St. Andrews Church in Park Walk to be set up behind her coffin which had been squeezed up the narrow staircase with great difficulty and into the best-room. It was then placed upon two trestles which stood in the centre of the room, the lid was removed, the candles were lit, and there she lay with the strong smell of the incense all around her. Over the next few days she would be visited by many of her large family, and a great many friends and neighbours, who would all come to say their last goodbyes.

I found the whole experience very special, and would pop in to sit with her on many occasions. She looked just as though she was sleeping, and her lovely old face still held a smile. There was nothing creepy or scary about her, and why should there be, for as she had often said herself, 'They didn't harm you when they was alive, and they won't harm you now they're dead'.

Her turn had now come to be the name at the top of the Sheet. The collection was made, and her neighbours contributed the grand total of £9.60 of the new decimal currency, to buy her flowers and pay their respects to one of their own.

Her funeral day arrived, and with all of her large family squeezed into the small sitting-room of our house we awaited the return of the undertakers who now had the task of bringing her coffin back down the narrow staircase. This was an awkward job and to do this the coffin, in order to turn a sharp corner on the staircase, would have to be lifted into an almost vertical position. As the undertakers raised it up all of us who were gathered downstairs waited for the small bump made by Gran as her body slid down to rest against the base of the coffin; this would be her final movement. Her funeral was well attended, with many people gathered in the street to see her on her way for the short journey to the Brompton Cemetery where, surrounded by all the elements of her now large family, she was laid to rest, to be finally reunited with her husband, William.

CHAPTER TWO

DEAD-END STREET

Life in a dead-end street is really quite different to any other street life, for having no thoroughfare all that goes on there is bottled up in a kind of vacuum, making everyone, and indeed everything, highly visible. This makes the keeping of secrets almost impossible but does create extremely close relationships, mostly good, but inevitably, some bad.

Our street was Slaidburn Street. The narrow three storey houses were built in the 1870s, and comprised of nine smallish rooms into which up to three families, sometimes totalling as many as twenty-five people, would squeeze themselves, all sharing the same ground-floor scullery which served as a washroom-cum-kitchen, through which access was gained to the small back-yard, which contained the one and only outside toilet.

All of the streets surrounding the old Worlds End were tough, but Slaidburn Street was arguably the toughest or roughest of them all, due I suppose to the fact that it was a dead-end street, making it easy to get into but not so easy to get out of. This gave it a natural protection that also worked as a strong deterrent to anyone, including the police, thinking of paying us a visit. Such was the reputation of our street that the Chelsea police were under strict orders to only enter it in strong numbers, having learnt their lesson some time during the 1930s when one cocky copper, having thrown his weight around just a little too much, was to have an experience that would be very hard to forget. Having aroused their anger, a bunch of the Street's tough guys easily overpowered him, the heavy iron cover was removed from one of the drains in the road, and down he went, head-first, helmet and all, with just his hobnail-boots visible kicking frantically in the air. There he was left for some hours before eventually being rescued by a large number of his fellow coppers. This story, unlikely though it sounds, was confirmed to me in the 1980s by a retired Chelsea policeman who, as a young man, had started his career as a bobby on the beat of the Worlds End. He knew most of the local characters and told me that the Worlds End was the favoured hangout of many street bookmakers. Street gambling was an offence back then, and so the police would try, mostly unsuccessfully, to catch them in the act, even entering the area concealed on the top deck of double-decker buses; but the bookies were nearly always one step ahead, and so would usually escape.

   The street was filled with a great assortment of characters of many different backgrounds and nationalities: Irish, Welsh, Polish and Scots, to mention but a few, and this would guarantee that it was always busy and full of life. Apart from the many kids up to their usual tricks, there were a large number of grannies who were part of the extended families that lived in most of the houses. Some had their own particular perches, others gathered in groups, chattering away about their favourite subjects, which, more often than not were of a morbid nature: who was ill, who had died, who had done what to who, etc.

   Being born Victorians, they all shared a fearful dread of anything medical: about hospitals they would say, 'Don't let 'em get yer in there, you'll never come out.' Or, about operations, 'Once they open you up you've had it. When the air gets at it, that's yer lot.' Others would spend the entire day leaning out of their windows, waving at and greeting neighbours as they passed on their way to work or, 'up the shops', as shopping was known. On warm days they would have chairs brought out for them and would sit sunning themselves, always managing to show the tops of their stockings which were held up by elastic bands just above the knee. They, like all the women, wore printed, floral, cotton smocks, and some days when carrying out particular chores such as polishing their front step, they would wear an additional apron on top.

Warm, sunny Sundays would really bring the street to life, as being a Sunday most people were at home and this gave them the opportunity to create their own entertainment outside. Of course, all the old ladies would be there, but on this occasion would be joined by groups of men who would sit around playing cards, usually for money. Us kids would indulge in our own form of gambling, playing 'Penny up the Wall', the object of which was to toss a penny from the edge of the pavement and try to land it as close to the wall of the house as possible. It was winner takes all, so the closest thrower would pocket all the coins.

Late afternoon we would be given money to buy blocks of ice-cream and bottles of lemonade with which were made ice-cream floats (a chunk of ice-cream in a glass topped up with lemonade). They were fab. More ice-cream would follow with the inevitable visit of Mr Remo in his ice-cream van with its strange horn which sounded just like a belching cow. Of course, we all got more ice-cream: tubs, cornets, lollies, or my favourite, a '99' (a cornet with a chocolate flake stuck in the top). On particularly good days we could be on the street as late as midnight.

There were always prams on the street surrounded by groups of housewives, all 'oohing' and 'aahing' over the Street's youngest members, between their bouts of house-work and cooking. All the food was home-made, for packaged meals were non-existent and there was no such thing as additives and E-numbers, they simply did not exist - so all food was real food. Our mothers would make wonderful pies, puddings, toad-in-the-hole, stew and dumplings, all kinds of wonderful desserts, and even home-made toffee. Mrs Beaton eat your heart out.

Billie Lowe lived in number 14, and, just like his hero Little Richard, was a real character. He was a small, wiry man, with a huge hooked nose, from which there was always suspended a dew-drop. He lived with his older brother Frank at number 14, and the two of them were the most gifted mechanics I have ever met: between them were capable of repairing just about anything.

The ground-floor of the house in which they lived was more of a workshop than a home, and on the rare occasion that I was able to gain entry I saw the most incredible collection of ancient TVs, stacked one upon another, washing-machines, and a huge collection of car parts, including entire engines, and being a bachelor pad it also included a mountainous stack of girlie magazines. Frank Lowe was the first person in our street to own a car. This car was hand-built by the brothers, and as such was unique. Frank had also built and flown his own light-aircraft, which was an amazing feat for this quiet and simple man. The aircraft had been confiscated at the beginning of World War Two.

Bill was Cyril's mechanic and carried out all the work on even his brand new cars. You would find him working in the street in even the coldest winters, and being the small, wiry man that he was, he would often sit cross-legged inside the engine compartment, working contentedly away, with the perpetual drip hanging from his long, thin nose. When he had finished working on the car he would take it for a test-drive, and upon his return would come into our sitting-room to announce in his usual distinctive way, 'It goes like a bomb, Cywil.'.

He never used a chair whilst in his greasy work clothes, and would crouch down on the floor to be served a glass of his favourite tipple, which was cherry brandy, a bottle being kept at home especially for him. Bill, unfortunately, died in his early fifties having contracted bronchitis, and was found early one morning by his brother Frank, dead on the stairs, having tried, but failed, to make it to his bedroom. Cyril was heart-broken, for he had a real soft spot for Bill, and as was his custom, accompanied by myself, off we went to the undertaker in Battersea to say our final goodbye. Having arrived we were shown into the room, and led by the undertaker to his coffin. There Bill lay, wearing his one and only suit that we knew so well from his many appearances at all our parties, but the face looking up at us was not so familiar. Unfortunately the undertakers had been a little over zealous with their make-up; his cheeks, which were usually adorned with a smudge or two of engine oil and grease, were now covered with so much rouge that they shone like apples. Cyril looked down on him, and with a tear in his eye remarked, 'Well, Bill, you look better now than you ever did alive.' He added, 'Ta ta Bill.' ... and off we went.

Frank died some years later, rather fittingly whilst driving his beloved car. He had a heart attack, and the car, with him at the wheel, came to rest right outside Chelsea football ground, the graveyard of many dreams.

On the top floor of number 16, the house next to ours, lived someone who we called Mad Gertie. Gertie was in her early forties and lived with her aged mother when not incarcerated in the Banstead Mental Hospital. She would often sit in the street chopping firewood with a small but very sharp hand-axe. One day when returning from work Cyril, feeling a little concerned by this unstable woman chopping away with an axe in a street full of kids, confronted her. This was a big mistake, for no sooner had he asked her to chop the wood in her back-yard than she turned on him, raised the axe and with wild eyes, chased him up and out of the street. Cyril was no coward, but realised that he was no match for this very wild woman, let alone armed with an axe.

On another occasion whilst playing football in the street, a bunch of us kids were surprised by the sudden appearance from the sky of a birdcage, complete with budgie. For reasons known only to herself, Mad Gertie had decided to throw it out of her third-floor window. Fortunately it crashed into the road missing everyone, but the birdseed and the feathers of the unfortunate budgie were sent flying all over the road. Incredibly the budgie though a little rattled, managed to survive.

Her most disturbing behaviour would always occur in the middle of the night when she would often go completely crazy, attacking her mother and waking the whole street with a volley of filthy language. The police were always called, for the screams of her mother were quite terrible. But more often than not, upon their arrival she would turn into the most placid and saintly person, leaving the police with little option but to leave her, for, as they told us, they could only intervene if they caught her in one of her frenzies. Of course, her mother always stood by her denying any harm being done, even though at times she had been attacked quite badly.

On very rare occasions her tortured mind would build up such a fury that she would be quite unable to turn it off. When this happened an ambulance would arrive from the mental hospital and a great fight would ensue. It always took several men to subdue her, for when she was out of control her strength was quite incredible. Eventually she would be brought out in a strait-jacket, her mother wailing behind her, and off she would go, only to return some weeks later, supposedly cured ... cured by what one can only wonder.

Strangely, Mad Gertie had a genuine liking for some children, my sister Carol being one - she would even buy her sweets - but she never took to adults. The mind boggles at what kind of childhood she herself had suffered to cause her madness. Upon the death of her old mother she was taken away and institutionalised, thankfully never to return to our street.

Lizzie Cook

Number 4 Slaidburn Street was always distinguishable by the round, dirt mark which was upon the wall to the side of its front door. This had been made by Lizzie Cook, a tiny but very tough little lady with bulging eyes and wild hair, who lived there with her family. Most of us kids were a little wary of Lizzie, for she wasn't afraid to give you a good rollicking in her crude and, at times, quite obscene language; or if she could get close enough she might even give you a clout. She, of course, wore the same type of floral, printed cotton smock like all the ladies in the street but, unlike them, hers would never be washed; somewhere behind the grime you could just make out the faintest impression of the once clear pattern. She would spend long hours upon her doorstep, standing with her arms crossed, leaning against the wall, and her dirty clothes over many years had indeed left their mark.

There was something Dickensian about this tough little Londoner who would not have been at all out of place in any of Dickens' stories, and just like many of his characters she was also illiterate. Upon her death it was discovered that the bath, which had been installed some years previously, was filled with coal; so it would seem that just like her clothes, Lizzie herself was not one for washing.

Number 23 was the home of the Smith family and at its head was the strong but diminutive figure of Stan. Stan ran the Chelsea Boys Club, which was situated in the basement of the old police station adjacent to The Globe Pub (later to become The Water Rat), which itself backed onto the mysterious Moravian Cemetery on the Kings Road. Inside the boys' club we would play snooker, table tennis and darts, or train in the gym for the club's football or boxing teams. Most kids were taught to box in those days, as it was generally thought that you were not safe unless you could handle yourself, so down in the sweaty gym we were taught to punch our weight by the boxing trainer who was a friend of Cyril's, called Len. Stan did a great job running the club, and all of us Chelsea boys will always be in his debt.

Right at the bottom of the street was number 30, inside which lived two elderly Irish brothers who were only ever known to us as the Paddies. This was actually their names and did not in any way refer to the fact of their being Irish which, of course, being London, would also make them Paddies. These two lovely and gentle old boys devoted their lives to the rescue of, and caring for, animals. They were always dressed rather shabbily in their ancient old clothes that had certainly seen better days, but obviously not for many years. One could only assume that they considered spending money upon anything other than animal care totally wasteful. The older Paddy was rarely seen and spent almost all of his time inside their home, caring for the many inmates that were always residing there. The younger Paddy, being only in his early seventies, would be far more familiar to us all, as he spent every day walking the streets of London looking for casualties. He was, as you would expect, a very gentle soul with a lovely old face. The skin was wrinkled with age but beautifully soft, and was finished off by two of what could only be described as blue Irish eyes, and yes, they were always smiling.

Whenever he appeared on the street he would be immediately surrounded by great numbers of pigeons and sparrows, who would land all over him to be fed handfuls of the dried corn that he always carried in the pockets of his old grey overcoat which, in cold weather, he would tie up with string. All of us kids were fascinated by his natural affinity with the birds, but no matter how hard we tried, or indeed, however much food we used to encourage them, we were never able to get the birds to repeat this performance, for it seemed that they only trusted the saint-like Paddy.

Upon the death of the two brothers in the 1970s, their home was to become, although only briefly, the scene of a murder mystery, much to the shock of the workmen who were there carrying out the long-overdue and much-needed repairs to what had been a rather unorthodox animal hospital. One day they all came running out of the house in quite a state, and word soon went round the street that they had found a body. It seems that when digging under the floor in one of the rooms they had come across a pile of bones, which they, not being qualified in such matters, assumed to be human. The police were called, and duly arrived to carry away the grisly remains, which were all bagged and sealed very tightly. Well, as you can imagine, this mystery created quite a stir in our little street, as none of us could believe that our two Paddies were anything other than the gentle souls that we had all known them to be. A short time after, the much relieved workmen were allowed to resume working on the house as, after examination, the bones were found to be those of a long-deceased donkey, that could only have been buried there by the builders of the street in the 1870s. What a strange coincidence it turned out to be that these two gentle old souls had unknowingly lived out their days above the grave of one of their much-loved animals.

There were many other animals in our street - and I don't mean the neighbours - but an assortment of different creatures, some destined for the pot but the great majority being pets. We ourselves had dogs, which would always be mongrels but with the required Labrador bit in there somewhere. They were always bitches and were, again, always named Tommy - a curious choice for a girl dog - but, I suppose, we were more than a little curious ourselves. The value of a dog in our lives is impossible to calculate, and I, for one, cannot imagine childhood without our best friend as one of the family. All of our Tommys, though similar types of dog, were quite unique in character.

    The first Tommy would allow anyone into the house, but getting back out was quite another matter, as our landlord, a small Jewish man by the name of Goldplumb, would find out. One day, he called to collect the rent, and having knocked and received no answer, decided to enter the house. He was greeted by Tommy who, with tail wagging, was friendliness itself, but this would change when he tried to leave. Gone was the wagging tail, to be replaced by a sinister growl with the baring of teeth, and there she sat, right in front of the entrance door, and refused to budge. After about half an hour my mother returned from shopping to find the pale-faced landlord, his back pinned up against the wall, greatly relieved but also very angry. He ranted at my mother about her dangerous dog, but only received a further lashing from her, as she told him that he had no right to enter our home and was lucky that he hadn't been bitten, and, in fact, it would have served him right if he had been. He rushed from our house, and after that employed someone else to collect his rents in Slaidburn Street.

    Our second Tommy just like Cyril, was rather fond of a tipple, so much so that she even had her own bowl at The Weatherby Arms at the top of our street. When you looked into the public bar you would see a long line of men sat on bar-stools, at the end of which would be Tommy, lapping beer from her bowl or munching on a large round dog biscuit. She always had a half, and was included in most of the rounds. One night, Cyril wobbled into our front room, after what had obviously been quite a night. My mother was not amused and casting him an angry look asked, 'Where's Tommy?'

    'Oh, she's coming', he sheepishly slurred. Leaving Cyril swaying in the room as if in a breeze, out we all went to look up the street, and there still some way off was the little dark shape of poor old Tommy, her legs going in all directions, as she attempted to wind her crooked path home. By the time she arrived Cyril had sidled off to bed to avoid the wrath of my mother for he knew only too well that he was now well and truly in the dog-house of his own making, and poor old Tommy was herself put to bed in her favourite armchair to sleep it off.

Tommy three was different from her predecessors, for she, unlike them, was an accomplished escape artist and a wanderer who would always manage to disappear from the house whenever the fancy took her. She would sometimes be gone for a number of days at a time to God only knows where, but she never failed to return, usually with a surprise package growing in her belly. On a couple of occasions, while waiting for a number 11 bus to take me off to school, I saw her familiar shape with tail wagging, come trotting along the Kings Road. She would sit and wait at the zebra-crossing for a car to stop, then trot over the road to stand by the bus stop opposite; a number 31 drew up and then, to my amazement, I watched as through the back window the outline of her little black body disappeared up the stairs to the top deck. Off went the bus with Tommy on board who, as yet, had not been seen by the conductor. Where she went to we never did know, but on both the occasions that I saw her do this, whether by accident or design, she happened to board a number 31.

The eventual outcome of all her wandering would take us on one of the most magical journeys that I remember from my childhood - PUPPIES! All of our Tommys had pups, as my mother insisted that it was harmful for them not to, so over the years many litters were born in our house. We all waited with growing anticipation as their bellies began to swell, and eventually one night we would be roused from our sleep, whatever the time (they always seemed to have their litters at night) to sit and watch the whole process. Tommy would select a corner of the room and start making a bed; then, with Cyril down on his knees in his role of midwife, the action would begin. Out they came one after another, tiny little pink creatures, more like mice than dogs, to be immediately licked clean by their mother, as we all stood watching and counting. Cyril, who was a big man, tenderly helped out if there was need; he always carried out his role as midwife beautifully. Over the next eight weeks the tiny mouse-like creatures would rapidly turn into a rampaging mob of hungry pups, all with individual colouring and characters. They were a great sight all lined up at the 'milk bar', as we called it, though poor old Tommy found it all a bit much especially when their small razor sharp teeth began to grow. There would always be a favourite, which was usually the runt of the litter, for being the smallest it was guaranteed to get the most attention from all of us. The largest litter that we had over the years was ten; this would require a great deal of attention and patience from us all to bring them through to the time when they could be packed off with their new masters to homes of their own. We never failed to place the pups, but all potential owners had first to pass the vetting which our mother always gave them. If for any reason she didn't like them she would send them off empty-handed and wait for the right people to appear, which incredibly they always did.

During the latter part of the 'Sixties, my sister Sue, along with her friend Maureen, had a part-time job of walking two dogs which were owned by the singer P.J. Proby - of the split pants fame. At this time he was rather down on his luck and was even struggling to find enough money to feed the dogs. Sue wasn't having this, so she asked Cyril if he could help out. He immediately agreed to do what he could and told Sue to bring P.J. to see him. Early one afternoon P.J., along with his massive St Bernard, who was called Buckingham, were sat in our little sitting-room. It was a memorable sight, Cyril in his usual suit and tie, his hair Brylcreemed as ever, P.J. had foregone his usual velvet suit and colour-matched buckle-shoes for the more casual attire of jeans and an open necked shirt but he still wore his long dark hair tied back with a ribbon into his familiar pony-tail. The big Texan and the big Londoner got on famously, and after a good chat Cyril presented P.J. with £20 and a bottle of Scotch, ordering him to: 'Make sure you spend that money on food for your dogs and not on booze.'

To this P.J. replied in his deep Texan voice, 'Well, thank you so much Mr. Devenport, I sure will.' And off he went.

All the houses in the street had a small back yard, and at the far end was situated the only, and much dreaded, outdoor toilet - not a nice place on cold winter nights - and it was in the small yard that people kept other kinds of animals. Along the street at number 15 lived my Uncle Frank and Aunt Emma. Uncle Frank who, due to his large ears was known as Dumbo, bred budgies, for which he had built a long chicken-wire-covered enclosure; this, at times, would hold up to thirty birds. Budgies were a popular pet back then, being pretty, cheerful, and most importantly, easy and cheap to own, so Uncle Frank did quite well from their sales which must have been a great help to support his strong gambling habit.

Some people would keep rabbits or chickens in their back-yard, this was the case with one of my mates Bone, or Tony Gibbons who lived at number 54. His father, Pat, would rear the chickens until they were deemed ready for the pot and he would then kill them by chopping off their heads with an axe; and, yes, they did run around the yard headless, which was a fascinating but rather unpleasant sight for all of us street kids, who would always gather to watch the grisly show.

At the top of the street there was a fruit and veg. seller called Mrs Rawlings. She was a small, tough but kind and friendly lady who meticulously laid out her produce every day upon a large barrow which was wheeled out from its shed just across the street from her home. The Rawlings family lived in number 3, and many of them helped out on the barrow at various times, including Ned, a good friend of Cyril's, who, in the mid-'Sixties, was to open up his own shop just a little way along the Kings Road.

There was a shop at number 47 run by another small lady called Mrs Christmas. Her shop sold mostly groceries and sweets, but of course also included cigarettes and tobacco. She was a friendly old soul, and from her it was possible to buy any amount of any of the many things that she stocked: one cigarette, an ounce of butter, a cup of sugar, an Oxo cube, or loose tea which she scooped out from large, foil-lined tea-chests to weigh on her scales. She would then wrap it, like most other things, in a simple brown-paper bag which was, and still is, the most minimal and by far most sensible form of packaging.

When Mrs Christmas died, her daughter, who had the delightful name of Ivy Christmas, chose not to step into her mother's shoes, and so the little shop closed; but it was soon taken on by Cyril who turned it into his workshop-cum-paint and wallpaper store.

On occasion we were also visited by various people who worked as street traders. There were knife sharpeners, furniture repairers, and then there was Nelly Ambo. Nelly was another throwback to Dickensian London: in her old clothes, her dress almost touching the ground and with a bonnet upon her head, she would push a hand-cart around the streets collecting rags and all sorts of junk. She would then return to the far end of Worlds End Passage to her small shop, which was filled with as odd an assortment of items as you could wish to see: matches, string, candles, all sorts of bric-a-brac, and even some items of food. Where it all came from one can only wonder, but she did manage to make some kind of a living by selling the odd item here and there. Her food, for obvious reasons, was something that was best avoided and its reputation was such that Nelly had her very own street song composed for her, which we kids would rather cruelly sing to her as she passed our way. It went like this:

> *Nelly Ambo sells fish*
> *Three ha'pence a dish;*
> *Don't try it, don't buy it,*
> *It smells when you fry it.*

Nelly was not alone in her chosen profession for the street would often be visited by rag-and-bone men who would appear upon their horse-drawn carts, announcing their presence with a long drawn out wail which went something like this: 'Ayennyoleion', which translates, though you'd never know it, to: 'Any old iron.' There were several junk shops around the Worlds End, some with yards where the horse and cart were kept, just like in Steptoe and Son, and one in particular was, I have always believed, to be the inspiration for that series; it was owned and run by a guy called John Fennell. This may not be as unlikely as it sounds for the writer Johnny Speight, just like so many of his profession, was naturally drawn to Chelsea, and a character such as John Fennel who was also a ringer for Harry H Corbett, must surely have caught his eye. Apart from being a popular and friendly guy he also happened to be just about the toughest guy in the Worlds End, which is really saying something, but although he was never one to look for trouble his reputation went before him, so unfortunately trouble was something that came to him. There was only one occasion that I remember John even struggling in a fight, and this was against three men, one armed with a machete, who attacked him right outside The Worlds End pub. Even three of them still couldn't put him down, for his head was literally like iron, but he did eventually succumb to gravity. This, however, was not from the best efforts of his attackers; it took a passing taxi whose path he had staggered into, to uproot this very tough man. In the early seventies he, like many others, would visit America for the first time, and while on holiday in Miami this tough and likeable Chelsea boy met a lady of some resources. Now John, just like many a Londoner, was a master of the art of blagging, and had told his American lady friend that he owned and ran an antiques shop in Chelsea. Well there was some truth in his story for his shop was in Chelsea, but a junk shop was a long way from an antique shop by any stretch of the imagination, and this would come back to haunt him. Having stayed in touch with his lady friend, one day she telephoned to announce that she was coming over to see him. This put the big tough guy into quite a state, and he found himself in a bit of a hole - all of course of his own making. After many failed attempts to put her off, or at least delay her visit, John spent a frenzied few weeks attempting the impossible, which was to make his run-down old shop with its yard full of scrap look half presentable before she arrived. What he told her on their way to Chelsea from the airport we can only guess, but what we do know is that the lady was not put off John in the least, and so, just like any good story which must have a happy ending, so it was to be with this one, as shortly after John would leave Chelsea for a new life in the warmer climes of Florida, and there he married his good lady.

  Saturday nights around the Worlds End were certainly never dull, especially after the closing time of the many busy pubs in the area. Often this would result in a none too pleasant, but always amusing, piece of street-theatre, as the drunken men, having stayed out longer than their allotted time, would stagger down the street, having had a' luvverly' time, but unwisely advertising their progress to all and sundry with their slurred and drunken singing. Upon arrival at their doorstep things would suddenly change, as being unable to open their front door, the realisation of being locked out would slowly sink in, and then a different kind of fun would begin.

It always began quite innocently with the man, his tail now firmly tucked between his legs, gently knocking at the door, and pleading through the letterbox, but receiving no response the volume of his pleas would inevitably rise; this would then result in one of the upper windows opening, which signalled the start of the slanging match for all in the street to hear. On many occasions this would quickly escalate with insults, threats and much swearing flying back and forth, but would usually result in victory for the besieged wife as she brought out the big guns, and rained down pots, pans and anything else that came to hand, sending the drunken husband into full retreat. After a short truce, with all their fire now spent, the door was usually opened, and the defeated male would skulk in to spend the next few days in the inevitable 'dog-house', as shamed exile was then known.

In those days the pubs were mostly male strongholds, though occasionally women could be found in the more comfortable saloon bar with its soft seats and carpet which all the pubs had then; but the public bar, with its wooden seats and floor, was strictly boys only - well, most of the time. The exception to this rule usually involved one or other of the men who having pushed his luck a bit too far and therefore being late for dinner, getting a visit from his none too happy wife ... and this was just the case with not only my own parents, but also my sister Sue, and her unfortunate husband Ray.

Both times involved Sunday lunch and the men's non-appearance at the table which, in Cyril's case, resulted in my mother Joyce doing a bit of waitressing. Eventually giving up on Cyril, and by now having built up quite a head of steam, she set off with the plated Sunday roast, with extra lashings of gravy, to stomp the 200 yards up the street to The Weatherby Arms. She flew through the double swinging- doors, made a bee-line for Cyril, and threw the whole plate at him, managing not only to cover him, but also doing a good job of covering most of his mates, who all shrank back, knowing better than to tackle a woman scorned - especially one like my mother. Some years later sister Sue, having run out of patience waiting at home for her other half, Ray, to put in an appearance for Sunday lunch, set off for the very same pub, armed with a pram and her two young children. As ever, right outside the pub was Ray's Jag. Sue stormed into the public bar and shoved the pram, kids and all, right up against Ray, pinning him to the bar, saying, 'I've had just about enough!' She then turned and left, leaving him well and truly lumbered with the kids, pram and all, surrounded by his now hysterical mates.

The winter of '62 - '63 was a memorable one indeed, for that was the only time in my memory that the Kings Road would be brought to a complete stop by that most unusual of things in London - snow. There was so much of it that us kids were able to roll a snowball from Stanley Bridge, the half mile or so along the Kings Road, now silent and bereft of traffic, all the way down to the Worlds End and into Slaidburn Street, by which time it had grown to be around six feet high. Boy, it was cold. This would also be the time when our notorious street with its eclectic mix of characters would be visited by a bunch of young guys, who in their time would attract their very own form of notoriety.

It was during this cold spell that The Weatherby, would for a short time figure in the journey of a group of unknown musicians who were on their way to become part of Rock and Roll history. Late in 1962 a rumour went around the Worlds End that The Beatles had moved into a flat just around the corner in Edith Grove. The Beatles were right at the beginning of their meteoric rise to global fame, and the pop scene as we now know it was still in its infancy. It didn't take us long to find out that it was not the Fab Four that were living in our back yard; they had only been there to pay a visit to the as yet unheard of bunch of fellow-rockers, called the Rolling Stones. I remember racing home with my sister Sue to share the earth-shattering news with our mum, 'Mum, the Rolling Stones are living around the corner!' we announced, with great excitement.

Being totally unmoved by our announcement she casually replied, 'A rolling stone gathers no moss.', and went back to her housework. This was the first time that I had heard this quote, but it would not be the last.

Their shabby flat at number 102 Edith Grove was very much inside the boundary of the rough and tough Worlds End and, just like any other newcomers to our patch, they would have to face their own particular initiation. Day after day they had to run the cauldron of all the streetwise kids who, upon seeing this bunch of long-haired beatniks in their sloppy joes, would taunt them with shouts of, 'Get your hair cut!' or, another favourite, 'Soap and water!' - because, in all honesty, they did look like a good wash-and-brush-up wouldn't do them any harm - after all, it only cost a shilling at the local public toilets which were upon the traffic island right in the heart of the old Worlds End.

    Their dirty appearance, however, did little to deter the attention they got from many of the local girls, and one afternoon I was taken to their dingy sanctuary by my attractive sister Carol. All I remember of that day was that there were a lot of people there, and the place was a chaotic mess: dirty plates and glasses littered the floor and piles of cigarette ends covered almost every conceivable surface. That was to be the only time that I would make it inside, for when, only a few days later whilst searching for Carol I hammered on the door, I was confronted by a none too happy Brian Jones, who even then stood out as the real dandy of the band. He looked down at me through bloodshot eyes and uttered the memorable words, 'Fuck off sonny!' and slammed the door in my face. He was never my favourite after that, but hey, who needed the Stones when you already had the Beatles.

    Many times the Stones would eat in the local greasy spoon, a little cafe just across the Kings Road from the aforementioned public loos. They were so hard up at this time that, even in this cheapest of cheap establishment, they were often seen to share three breakfasts between the five, and sometimes the six of them. Their meals were always rushed, for, just like out on the streets, they would have to face more taunts from the much sturdier local dustmen, rag-and-bone-men and builders, whose territory they had dared to enter.

    The Stones rehearsed in The Weatherby Arms on the corner of our street which, conveniently for them, was no more than a stones throw from their shabby flat, but more importantly, the pub also had an old wooden-floored function room off the public bar with a gated side entrance going into Slaidburn Street. One night in May, with the cold winter now thankfully behind us, I sat with a bunch of friends in the side entrance to listen as they rehearsed. But this was no ordinary rehearsal, for that night they played just one song, repeating it over and over again, tweaking it and striving to perfect it, for the next day they were off across town to Olympic Sound Studios near Marble Arch to record what was to be their first proper record, the Chuck Berry song 'Come On'. Now, The Weatherby was by far the roughest pub in the Worlds End, and the Stones would have to rehearse to the rowdy accompaniment of the crowd of working men, which included Cyril, along with our dog Tommy with her own beer bowl, in the adjoining public bar. That particular night the accompaniment went something like this: 'What a bleeding racket! Don't you know any other songs? You call that singing!' etc. etc. Needless to say these did not make it onto the record.

   Things then moved pretty fast for the Stones, with just more than a little help from their new friends the Beatles. Any contact with the Beatles was almost guaranteed to reap rewards and, just like many other bands at the time, the Stones were also to benefit from the stardust that seemed to stick to all they touched. The generosity and prolific output of the 'Mop Tops' was such that they would not only write the Stones second single and first hit 'I Wanna be your Man', but would also inspire them to write all of their own material - this was something that the Stones were to do from that time on. Just as we were getting used to having the Stones around and had almost accepted them as Worlds Enders, their own, by now meteoric rise, would signal the time for them to leave us. I'm sure that they were greatly relieved as they packed their bags and departed for the more genteel, not to mention more upmarket parts of Chelsea. ... And as they say, the rest is history.

CHAPTER THREE

THE REFORMED MONARCHIST

As Cyril began to build his business he was faced with the difficult task of finding the right kind of men with the required skills to carry out the many tasks of a London builder. He was most fortunate to come across, and have as one of his first full-time employees, a tough but very likeable chap called Bill Marriott. Bill was an old-fashioned Londoner, short and stocky, with a flash of white running through his thick head of otherwise dark hair. He always wore an old dark suit which showed the signs of hard wear by its shiny patches around the knees and elbows, a white shirt open at the neck, for he never wore a tie, and over which would always be, summer or winter, a dark V-necked jumper, knitted for him by Mrs M. He was born in 1898 which, unfortunately, made him the perfect age and prime fodder for the outbreak of World War One in 1914.

Bill joined the Royal Horse Artillery, and was packed off to Europe to participate in the horror of what has to be one of the darkest times of the human race. Understandably, and like so many others, this terrible experience had a marked effect on young Bill, and it would be something which he was to carry with him for most of the rest of his life. Bill always felt, maybe accurately, that the monarchies of Europe had been largely responsible for the awful blood-letting that took place, and in this he had a good point, for three of the main players in this awful drama just happened to be cousins: our own King George V, Zsar Nicholas of Russia, and last but not least, the arrogant and extremely pompous Kaiser Willhelm II of Germany. As is well known, family squabbles can become very nasty, but these three between them would take the term 'family squabble' to undreamed of heights, and it was this, in effect, that would make the otherwise likeable down-to-earth Londoner into one of the most vehement anti-monarchists you were ever likely to meet.

Bill was to be the pillar around which Cyril would build his early business, and quite naturally was given the position of foreman, so putting him in charge of all the other men. Being a foreman in those days carried with it not only a great responsibility but also afforded the bearer with a certain status, placing him a cut above the rest of the working-men. This was something that was never too evident with Bill who was always popular with his work mates, but his successor some years later, another Bill coincidentally, would use his position quite differently, even removing himself to a separate room for tea and lunch breaks, considering getting too close to his charges as a threat to his status and authority. They were both first-class decorators, and as such carried the title of 'Silky', which meant that they would only be required to hang wallpaper, so avoiding much of the dirty work required in preparation. This would also allow them to work in slippers, something that was quite unique to them. I can only guess that the name 'Silky' referred to paperhangers having soft hands.

As a boy I was to see much of Bill who, like Cyril, was rather fond of a drink, and on many occasions they would meet up at various pubs where I, having persuaded Cyril to take me along, would sit in the car outside to be brought lemonade and crisps. Sneaking out occasionally I would peer through one of the windows to watch them through the smoky atmosphere of the bar, discussing work, and, of course, having a drink. This had obviously made quite an impression upon my young mind, for when he visited our home I would, without fail, go straight to the cocktail cabinet to present him with a bottle of whisky. This would happen even at eight in the morning! It always created roars of laughter, and my mother would say, 'He's got you taped Bill!' I would see him at work, or on many occasions drive across London with Cyril to visit Bill and Mrs Marriot at their home in a council flat on the very rough White City estate. This was always great fun, for Mrs M was a typical Cockney lady, generous and kind, and would treat me to tea and cakes, while Bill and Cyril sat chatting and supping their favoured whisky in the old-fashioned sitting-room.

Around 1963, Cyril, whose reputation had grown considerably by now, was to work at Windsor Castle, which was a real feather in his cap. The job was the redecoration of the Duke of Gloucester's apartments, for apart from the Queen's direct family many other minor royals also have residences in the palaces. This created a lot of head-scratching for Cyril, whose best decorator would now be inside one of the royal palaces, and Bill, being well into his sixties by now, had a mind set in stone with his low opinion of the Royals, and this was something he always relished getting his teeth into. Bill, like many men of that time, was also a smoker, and chose to roll his own tiny cigarettes, which being so thin, were known as panel-pins. These he would have constantly stuck to his bottom lip and they would often go out, so he would relight them when and as necessary. Now, smoking was a big 'no-no' in the palaces - well, it was for the working-class - but this definitely didn't apply to Bill, for as hard as Cyril tried to stop him Bill would just carry on puffing, and with a big grin on his face would state, 'What's good enough for them is good enough for me.' He relished this act of rebellion, so much so that he smoked all the more because of it.

Cyril visited the palace daily to both check the work and keep the men supplied with paints and papers. He always felt a great pride as he approached the very distinctive turreted shape that is Windsor Castle; it had been a hard journey, but now he had truly arrived. One such morning, Cyril, having done his rounds left the men and set off whistling in his usual happy manner, from the apartments. As he walked down a long corridor he saw approaching from the far end a group of ladies, and upon getting closer he realised to his alarm that amongst them was the Queen herself. …With a gulp his whistling came to an abrupt halt.

As the gap between them closed he was approached by a lady-in-waiting who enquired who he was. Having introduced himself, Cyril was then presented by the lady-in-waiting to the Queen. The Queen remarked that this was jolly good timing as she was herself on her way to inspect the work, and would Cyril please be kind enough to accompany her. Cyril replied that he would be delighted, but in his head the alarm bells were ringing loudly at the thought of H.M. and her confrontation with the monarchy-hating Bill M. He was then instructed to announce the Queen upon entering the apartments.

Cyril entered, and as instructed cried out in his best London voice, 'Gentlemen, Her Majesty!' This had no affect at all. The men just carried on as if to say, 'Oh yeah, Cyril, pull the other one.' But then, as the group of ladies entered the room, a stunned silence fell upon them all, as they realised that this time it was definitely not one of Cyril's jokes, for there, as large as life standing right next to him, was H.M. the Queen in the flesh. Cyril lined up the men who the Queen had expressed her wish to meet. There in the line stood Bill, panel-pin stuck, as ever, to his bottom lip. Cyril's knees began to wobble at this point, and then he felt especially faint as the Queen headed straight for Bill.

The Queen remarked, 'You are obviously the senior man here.' She commended him for the fine job that he was making, and then they began to chat. H.M. asked Bill if he had served in the forces. Cyril thought, Oh no, not the war - took a deep breath, and as time seemed to stand still, waited for the fire and brimstone to erupt from Bill's still panel-pinned lips. Then, to everyone's surprise, Bill politely replied, 'Yes Ma'am, I was in the Royal 'Orse Artillery'.

The Queen replied, 'Oh, that was my uncle's regiment. Do you still have an interest in horses?' Here, in one deft stroke, H.M., surely the most consummate of communicators, had turned the subject toward the one thing that they had in common, for as we all know, H.M., just like Bill, has always had rather a soft spot for the gee-gees. At this point the conversation turned into 'A Day at the Races', and they stood together swapping notes on the Derby, the National, the merits of the two most popular jockeys of the time, Lester Piggott and Scobie Breasley, and all things horsey. To say they got on famously would be an understatement, and all the while on the side lines stands Cyril, open-mouthed and completely speechless. Having regained his composure he then presents the rest of the men to the Queen, after which she then turns to Cyril and says, 'Thank you very much Mr Devenport.' - and accompanied by her ladies-in-waiting, departs the scene.

Cyril turns to Bill, but before he could say a word, Bill, with the panel pin still stuck to his bottom lip, looks straight back at him and says, 'What a luvverly lady.' - and for the second time that morning

Cyril leaves the room, with the men talking excitedly about what must have been quite an experience for them all – but for no one more so than Bill.

Shortly after this memorable day I went with Cyril for one of our usual visits to Bill and Mrs Marriott at their flat in White City. There we were to witness the remarkable effect that Bill's brief encounter with this extraordinary woman had had upon him. As we entered their small sitting-room it soon became obvious that things were not quite as before, for now, hanging from the wall above the fireplace, in pride of place in fact, was a huge portrait of the Queen, brand new, and smiling down over her now reformed subject ... who would remain an ardent monarchist for the rest of his days. Some years later we were to have another close encounter with a member of the Royal Family, and one, that had Bill been with us, may well have seen him change his mind once again.

In all the years of working with my father Cyril I was only to see a client take offence at his lightness of character once, and this was not just any client, for the client in question was none other than the sister of the Queen, Princess Margaret. That first visit to Kensington Palace was memorable in more ways than one for the Princess was all light and laughter as she gave Cyril and I a personal tour of her apartments pointing out along the way some of her many possessions accompanied with little anecdotes and all was fine until we entered her bedroom. As we followed the Princess at a respectable distance, her eye fell upon a bureau across the room and turning to Cyril she said, 'Ah Mr Devenport, you may find this interesting. This piece was made by my husband.'

Cyril moved forward to look closely at the bureau, and then turning to Margaret he said, 'Well Ma'am, it certainly is beautifully made. If your husband ever needs a job you can send him to see me.'

This was typical of Cyril, and was one of the reasons why so many people loved him, but alas, not the Princess, whose reaction was instantaneous. Her face filled with fury, and she turned about and stormed from the room leaving us both in a confused state, to find our own way out of her home. Surprisingly we still got to do the work in the Palace, although neither sight nor sound of Princess Margaret was ever seen by us again.

CHAPTER FOUR

I DO LIKE TO BE BESIDE THE SEASIDE

Outings were a great tradition for most Londoners, and as such were a popular way for the men or ladies, separately, of course, to get away from each other (this being an essential part of the plan) and have a thoroughly good day out. In our street these outings dated back to the late 1920s, when the men would set off for a boozy trip in wonderful open-top charabancs to some seaside destination. On the whole these were organised by the local pubs, so were known as pub outings. Cars were very scarce before the 1960s so the much looked forward to outings were always well attended as they created a welcome break for many Londoners from the intensity of their home life.

With the arrival of the coach at the pub all the kids would gather, to wait in great excitement for the ritual involved with its departure. The men would arrive dressed up in their Sunday best, wearing their one good suit, finished off with a hat. Hats were an essential item in those days, the men's being an assortment of caps, a few trilbies, and for the more daring amongst them, even the occasional beret. As soon as all the men were on the coach one of the numerous hats would be passed around, into which all their loose change would be placed in preparation for the traditional departure. The door would close, the engine would start, and as the coach pulled away the hat would appear from one of the rear windows with the familiar shout of: 'Scramble!' going up from all the men inside. Down would come the coins to clatter all over the street, and down went all us kids to fight furiously and grab as many coins as we could lay our hands on, as the men all crowded around the back window of the now departing coach to look back, laughing and waving.

The destination was always the seaside: Southend, Margate and Brighton were the favoured places, although there would be many stops before they were eventually to arrive. A typical outing would involve stopping at several pubs along the way, followed by lunch at their destination ... where else, but in another pub. After a short walk along the seafront, with the more adventurous of them even braving a stroll on the pier, they would depart for the drive home, stopping once again at many more pubs on the way back. As you can imagine, boys being boys, they were in quite a state when they eventually returned home, and were inevitably put in the much used dog-house by their respective wives.

Part of their penance would be to pay for the women's outing, of which there would usually be only the one annually; but the girls, being rather fond of a tipple themselves, would all have a great time. Unlike the men they would stop only once on the way there, and once again on the way back. On one such return trip my grandmother, Nell, would get quite a fright. The coach by this time being full of boozy ladies with their bladders bursting, was forced to stop for an inevitable emergency toilet-break. Nell was not exactly bashful, but was a rather private person when it came to toiletry, so, with all the ladies scrambling around in a dark field in order to find their own little patch, off she went. As it turned out she went just a little too far, and before she knew it she found herself sinking fast into an appropriately named bog. After much screaming she was eventually found, and dragged from what she thought was to be her final resting place. From that day on she had a great distrust of the countryside.

Lunch was had not at the pub like the men but at the Joe Lyons on the sea-front, or so they told us ... but I think the photograph of them tells quite a different story. Just like the men they all wore their best clothes, which were always finished off with their prize possessions: their best coat and hat, and yes, once again their departure would also involve the inevitable 'scramble'.

Of course, we kids had to have our turn. In our case this would involve the whole family piling into Cyril's Dormobile (an early kind of caravanette) - not quite a Winnebago - but hey, this is England! Off we'd go, to get lost as usual, somewhere in deepest, darkest Kent. Kent was popular for Londoners at the time, for it really was the garden of England, being packed with wonderful orchards full of many kinds of fruit, all very tempting and convenient for us townies who loved nothing better than a bit of scrumping. We would also visit the seaside: Margate and Ramsgate being the usual destinations. The seaside was really thriving in those days, and the beaches were absolutely packed with hoards of people, mostly Londoners, many with the archetypal pythonesque white hankie tied to their heads. Finding your own little piece of England upon the crowded sand was always a challenge, and kids who are always prone to wander would get lost in the large crowds all the time. To deal with this there were Tannoy loudspeakers placed high on poles along the beach, and through these the unfortunate strays would have to bear the great embarrassment of their names being blared out across the crowded sands for all to hear; they were taken to the first-aid hut and would eventually be collected by their parents. I was one such ... but only once.

Our first family holidays were spent like many Londoners at a caravan site in Leysdown, upon the Isle of Sheppey in Kent. Being a mere forty miles from London this made it easily accessible and a popular choice for many families. A whole troupe of us would go: uncles, aunts, cousins and neighbours, to spend a week together in the great outdoors. Almost everyone in the early 60s would take their holidays (if they had one at all) close to home, for being just fifteen years since the end of World War Two money was still short for most people, and holidays abroad were unimaginable and still some way off in the future. Most days were spent on the beach: playing games, flying kites or peering into rock-pools looking for crabs which, when we were lucky (although not so lucky for the crabs) would be brought back in a bucket to our caravan. There they would be unceremoniously thrown into a pan of boiling water whilst still alive, always giving off a little scream as they went in. This was all rather unpleasant, but was supposed to be the most humane way of dispatching them, though how that was ever worked out we will never know. The ghastly deed now forgotten we would all sit down to break up the shells to get at the sweet meat inside which, being so fresh, guaranteed that they were absolutely delicious. These were very simple holidays, and apart from much time spent walking near or on the beach, we would also visit the local towns to do a bit of shopping. There was a small clubhouse on the site, and, needless to say, most evenings were spent there with all the adults having a good booze-up and a good sing-song. After many 'Hokey Cokeys' and a few 'Gay Gordons' we would always end the night with the inevitable raucous 'Knees up Mother Brown'.

The next holidays I remember were spent at the Warners Holiday Camp, which was in a small town called Littlestone-on-Sea which, not surprisingly, was also in Kent. Holiday camps were the precursors of the later to come package-holidays, and for a short time in their boom years during the 1950s and 1960s would be the place where many of the working-class population would have their first proper vacations. Things for us were really looking up as Cyril's business went from strength to strength, so now we, like many others, could afford to spend our holidays in a proper resort with its many facilities, but even more importantly, we now stayed in chalets, which though far from luxurious were a great improvement upon small overcrowded caravans.

Holiday camps bore more than a passing resemblance to army camps, though I suppose this was inevitable considering the large number of people that they accommodated, all of whom had to be catered for, and this required a military-style type of organisation, which being such a short a time since the war was still much in evidence in Britain. However, unlike the army, all activities were voluntary, and though some were not without their danger they were obviously a lot more fun. The chalets were laid out in long lines, each having its own number, which would be called out when necessary over the public address system. This was a collection of large trumpet-like Tannoy speakers which were placed all around the camp, and were used to communicate all sorts of information to all the happy holidaymakers. The day would start around 7.30 a.m. with a trumpet blaring out 'Reveille'. It was a rude awakening, but very effective in waking even the soundest of sleepers - so there was no loafing in bed. It would be followed by one of the camp stewards who would announce: 'Morning, campers! Breakfast will be served for chalet numbers one to fifty at eight o'clock in the dining hall!' The whole process would be repeated for lunch and dinner ... it was all very 'Carry On' - and even Sergeant Bilko would have felt right at home. Who said the war was over?

   Our days would be spent mostly around the camp where you could hire three-seater bikes, which were basically two normal bikes joined side-by-side with a wooden seat in between. They were great fun, but the early ones could be a little dodgy going around corners, as I was soon to discover to my cost. I, being about six at the time, was sat between two of my sisters who, upon reaching a corner, decided to turn in opposite directions. This stopped the bike dead in its tracks, but alas not me, for I was propelled over the handlebars with my head coming to an abrupt stop against an unyielding brick wall. To their horror blood was now pouring from a cut above my left eye, so they snatched me up and raced me back to the chalet which we had left only a few short, but eventful minutes before. To say our mum was not happy would be an understatement, and she gave them a good roasting all the way to the hospital, where I was to receive several stitches.

   The camp also had a decent sized outdoor swimming pool which, for me with my stitched face, would be out of bounds; but this didn't stop the rest of the family from having a swim, or indeed, stop Cyril from giving us another of his quite unique displays. One afternoon we were all sat around the pool, which was quite crowded as it was a lovely sunny day. Cyril was getting on at the girls, taunting them to show him how good they were at diving, but this backfired, and being outnumbered and after much bullying from all of us, he ended up being the one who was going to show us how good he was at diving. Cyril was never really the athletic type, and I for one barely remembered him even swimming let alone diving, so with rapt attention we all watched as he strode to the edge of the crowded pool. He waited for a space to appear, and then, to the unbelieving gaze of us all, launched himself off into the air. Now, Cyril was a big man, and he hit the water dead flat, in what was called a belly-flop; this created a very loud slap which naturally attracted the attention of everyone there. Under the now much disturbed surface of the pool he went, to eventually surface, coughing and spluttering, water pouring out of his nose and mouth to head for the safety of the steps at the side. With the whole crowd still watching he began to climb out, and it soon became obvious that something was missing, for his clumsy dive had relieved him of his trunks, which were now resting peacefully on the bottom of the pool. He didn't bat an eyelid, he just turned, dived down to the bottom of the pool to retrieve them, and still coughing and spluttering he then slowly but awkwardly put them on again, and finally, casually climbed out to the cheers of everyone there. It was Cyril at his best, who in his own inimitable way had, as usual, embarrassed us far more than he had himself. Typical Cyril.

  On the seafront we were lucky to have a station for the Romney, Hythe and Dymchurch Railway. From the small station we would board one of the four-seater carriages, which were pulled by beautiful one-third-scale steam engines. These would take you for a wonderful ride along the Kent coast, stopping at nearby towns. It was a great way to spend a couple of hours. Thankfully, after being closed by the dreadful Dr. Beeching in the late 1960s, it has now returned to the Kent coast to once again thrill people with its chugging, puffing presence.

  Evenings at the camp would be spent in the large ballroom, where we were entertained by a collection of bands, some comedians - who tried, but were not always, funny – and, of course, the inevitable rabbit-from-a-hat-style magician. Much more fun was had when the audience was enticed to take part in various contests. These took place upon the wooden ballroom floor, and would include limbo, which was great fun (even though the girls always won), miniature-bike races, which always resulted in some crashes with a few bruises, and giant games of musical-chairs with a twist, for the chairs would be occupied by members of the opposite sex - the object being to find a vacant, and if you were lucky, attractive lap to sit on. The evening would always end with a spot of dancing – Jive, Waltz, the Twist, Gay Gordons, and once again, the inevitable 'Knees up Mother Brown' ... Who was this woman?

Looking back, they were simple holidays but were also thoroughly enjoyable, and, as with most things involving Cyril, they were also guaranteed to be a whole lot of fun.

It would be some years yet before we were to make it to foreign lands, but one of our family, probably the least likely of all, was to precede us overseas by some time. Aunty Ivy was Cyril's next eldest sister, and just like her little brother, was also quite a character. Ivy was a rather large, or traditionally built, lady, and was married to Tom Bannerstone, a tall, thin man, who during the war had served in North Africa with Montgomery's Eighth Army. Their language was always colourful: an earthy cockney, into which the inevitable swear word would fall quite naturally, being rather rude but never crude, and together they made quite a pair. Their physical attributes gave them more than a passing resemblance of a mixed sex Laurel and Hardy - and the similarities did not end there. I think it would be fair to say that Tom and Ivy were by far the poorest couple in our large extended family, but this in no way affected their personalities, for it was quite obvious that they were also the happiest. They say that life is what you make it, and between them these two would certainly make all our lives a richer place. Over the years Ivy would visit us at Slaidburn Street at least once a week, popping in usually in the late afternoon on her way home from work, or sometimes accompanied by Tom at the weekend. In the early days they would arrive together on Tom's motor bike with a side-car attached, inside which would be squeezed Aunty Ivy's considerable frame. As Uncle Tom climbed off, the bike would almost leave the ground, only to return when, after much heaving and pulling, Aunty Ivy was eventually pulled like a cork from a bottle from the enclosed side-car.

She always had a tale to tell, but the most interesting stories always came after one of their numerous holidays which, being members of the Caravan Club, they would take at home or abroad in their camper-van. Ivy would sit with a cup of tea, her skirt hoisted up, just showing the tops of her stockings, held up by elastic, which covered her large legs, and out would come her own version of the travel show from camp-sites all over Europe. She really liked Italy, for unlike us, the 'Eyeties', as she called them, were particularly fond of traditionally built women, and they, to her delight, were not afraid to show their approval, or as she put it, 'I had my bum pinched everywhere we went; it was lovely.'

Another trip was spent in Holland at the Caravan Clubs European Convention, where the caravanners from many countries were presented with a gift package from the organisers, which included a basket of fruit and an assortment of tulip bulbs. Tom and Ivy's camper-van happened to be next to that of a family from France, who in their very French way would give Ivy a great laugh as they prepared their evening meal, or as she put it herself, 'What do you think the fucking French did? - They only cooked the tulips 'cos they thought they was onions!'

For a short time they also had a small motor boat which, like most of their possessions, was a bit the worse for wear, and was only kept working by the ingenuity of Tom who had a natural talent for repairing things. One day, whilst out on the boat, Ivy fell overboard. Tom, after scrambling through the cluttered cabin, appeared back on deck with his improvised life buoy - a large tyre inner-tube. He threw it to the flailing Ivy who, with much effort, managed to squeeze it over her head and slowly down around her large body. All seemed well at first, but then suddenly gravity played its hand, and Ivy, being top heavy, tipped completely upside down. She must have made quite a spectacle with her huge bloomered bottom protruding from the improvised life buoy and her large legs swinging wildly in the air. Tom eventually righted her, and managed somehow to get her safely back on board, though, as she told us, ' He certainly took 'is time; I thought he was gonna let me drown!' Boy, did we all laugh, and, as ever, it was Ivy who laughed the loudest. Not long after this the boat sank, whether by accident or by Ivy's design we never did find out, but I know she was not too bothered to see its end.

Having reached sixty-five Ivy's large body had begun to show signs of wear and tear, which was most noticeable with the arthritis she suffered in her knees, but she still, remarkably, carried on her job as an office cleaner. Along with my four sisters a plan was hatched to help her out by us paying her wages, which we thought would relieve her of the necessity of having to work. Upon her next visit to Slaidburn Street we were, as was usual, all sat round chatting over a cup of tea, during which we told her of our plan. Ivy was rarely angry, but after hearing of our intentions she flew into a rage. 'Don't you try to stop me from working, I love my job! So, thank you and no thank you, and I'll ask you to keep your noses out of my business from now on.' We were gob-smacked, as, of course, we had only had her well-being in mind, but no one had realised until that day just how much of a part her work was already playing in that very role.

One afternoon, whilst visiting my mother, Ivy turned up for what was to turn out to be one of her last visits to our house, and she would, once again, have the whole place filled with laughter. Cup of tea in front of her, Ivy began to rummage in her handbag, giggling away to herself; she then produced a pack of photographs, going on to explain that she had done a treat for one of the offices that she cleaned, but only my mother could see the photos. Well, I wasn't having this, and a game of tug-of-war then ensued, with Ivy saying, 'Don't let him see - don't, stop it, you can't look!' Of course I did look, and as Ivy sat blushing and giggling, repeating over and over, 'Don't look!', my eyes nearly popped out, for in the photos there she was, dressed, or more accurately undressed, in black suspenders, knickers and a bra with scarlet edging, all finished off with fishnet stockings. Considering that she was in her late sixties she actually looked really good in her role of the strippogram, and being the good sport that she had always been had given all the people at the office party a great laugh.

I have always found famous last words most interesting, and one of my favourites has to be those spoken by King George V. Having been unwell for some time, his physician made the suggestion that His Majesty would soon be well enough to visit Bognor, to which the King replied, 'Bugger Bognor!' ... and promptly died. Aunty Ivy's last words would also be quite memorable.

In 1981 she was to suffer a stroke, and was rushed into what was then St. Stephens Hospital in Chelsea. Here she was to spend her last few days in a coma in intensive care, where all of her family were to visit her. One afternoon my mother Joyce, Ivy's daughter Dolly, two of my sisters and myself, were sat around her bed, talking amongst ourselves and including her in our chat, in the hope that she may be able to hear. Ivy had been a regular visitor to her local spiritualist church, and was also a friend and neighbour of the well-known spirit medium, Doris Stokes, who was appearing that week at the Dominion Theatre in London's West End. As we sat discussing her medium friend, Ivy, with her bandaged head, which made her appear as if she was wearing a turban, suddenly sat bolt upright in her bed and bellowed out in an incredibly loud voice which carried all around her particular floor of the hospital: 'BOLLOCKS!' We were stunned, and watched as she slowly descended peacefully back onto her pillow to once more return to her comatose state. She had certainly had the last word - for that is exactly what it turned out to be ... as she was to pass away the very next day.

It would now seem that Ivy's short but most precise contribution to our conversation that afternoon was rather well informed, for being as she was 'between worlds' so to speak, had given her access to information well beyond the reach of all of us. For it now appears that the carefully crafted act of her medium friend Doris was nothing more than what the larger than life Ivy had made so very clear all those years ago; in other words, it was all an absolute and complete load of bollocks.

Eventually my parents would inevitably make it overseas to visit many countries, among them being America, Russia, Sweden, Greece, and, upon one memorable occasion, Bulgaria. This trip was taken, along with a boyhood friend of Cyril's, a gentle giant of a man called Boy Sanneford. Boy cut a striking figure with his full head of blond hair added to which he stood 6 ft 6 in. tall, making him rather a big boy indeed. One night, Cyril and Boy, who were both more than a little fond of a drink were left, rather unwisely, alone in the hotel bar. Needless to say, the hours slipped away, and having downed many drinks and overstayed their allotted time they both staggered off to their rooms in the small hours of the morning. A few hours later my mother Joyce, who was still fuming having spent part of the night alongside a drunken, snoring Cyril, was sat alone in the hotel lobby, when the doors of the elevator opened to reveal Cyril's partner in crime, the very large and grey-looking Boy. Having spotted her and fearing the worst he took off across the lobby, but his escape was short-lived for he came to a crashing stop as he walked straight into a wall upon which stood a large mirror. My mother rushed over to the dazed and shaken Boy and asked him what had happened and if he was alright. He replied, 'I think so.' and rubbing his head went on to say, 'I thought he was going to get out of the way.' – It now became clear that he had mistaken the mirror for a doorway and so had walked smack into himself. With a satisfied look upon her face she then looked down at the fallen giant and said, 'It serves you bloody well right!' ... and left him there, still rubbing his now even sorer head.

CHAPTER FIVE

WE ARE THE CHELSEA BOYS

'We are the Chelsea Boys
We are the Chelsea Boys
We know all our manners
We spend all our tanners
We are respected wherever we go
Marching down the Old Kings Road
Doors and windows open wide
If you hear a copper shout
Put that tuppeny woodbine out
We are the Chelsea Boys'

This was one of the many street-songs that we as London kids sang, and this particular song, being about us Chelsea kids, would be the one that we sang more than all the others. Street-songs were a very important part of growing up in London; they would evolve quite naturally during the huge amount of time that we all spent out on the streets entertaining ourselves (or annoying others) with our many games, and all sorts of other interesting pursuits. These, on the whole, just like the songs, were passed from one generation to the next, or now and then new ones would be made up as we went along. Singing away, we would explore our home patch with the many attractions that we were lucky to have surrounding us in the Worlds End, which conveniently were all within the short space of a mile. There were the wonderful collection of museums at South Kensington, packed to the gills with dinosaurs, a Dodo, who even after the best efforts of the taxidermist still looked - well, as dead as a Dodo; and even the stuffed body of Mick the Miller, the famous greyhound ... indicating the great popularity of 'a night at the dogs', as greyhound racing was often called. There were more parks than you could wish for, including Battersea, with it's Fun Fair (of which more will be said later); Stamford Bridge, where we would watch not only football but dog racing; the ever present Thames, and being on the Kings Road gave us front row seats to watch the flowering of the beautiful people, with all the great shops that were to blossom there during the Swinging Sixties. All in all, not a bad place to be a kid.

My London of the 1950s and 60s was a much different place to the one that Cyril had grown up in where survival was the dominant factor, but boys were still boys and he, along with all his mates, would find many ways to entertain himself. One of these was really a kind of initiation, and a dangerous one at that, for all the boys at one time or another would be pressured by their peers to take a jump from Battersea Bridge into the dirty swirling water of the river Thames. Thankfully, this pursuit did not come through to my time.

London for me was really just one huge adventure playground: there were bomb sites and derelict houses everywhere, which were all much used by us kids lucky enough to grow up there at that time … it felt like the streets really did belong to us. There were very few cars (only two in Slaidburn Street), and the strength of local communities guaranteed our safety as the streets were always teeming with hordes of people, not just kids but plenty of adults as well: mums with babies in prams of all descriptions, and lots of grannies, who would sit on chairs outside their homes or hang out from their windows, chatting away to the many passers-by. Our lives then were really quite basic. Outdoor toilets were the norm, and for many a bath required a visit to the public baths in Chelsea Manor Street, which from the Worlds End was about half way towards the other more recognised posh end of Sloane Square – the Chelsea of the upper-classes, with all of their alluring affluence. From the Worlds End to the posh end was only the distance of about one mile straight along the busy Kings Road, but this was not the only way to travel between the two worlds. The other route was by the winding back-streets, which in those days, before the encroachment of the many one-way-systems, made it possible to go from one end of Chelsea to the other without ever touching the more conspicuous Kings Road. This was known, for obvious reasons, as 'The Burglars Route'.

The huge gap between the 'haves' and the 'have nots' in the two very different Chelsea's would create for us Worlds enders a most alluring environment of almost accepted opportunity to level the score a bit. Some of us kids, with ingenuity, cunning, and, it must be said, a certain amount of dishonesty, would use this to our advantage, finding many ways to supplement our meagre pocket-money in order to finance the many attractions which were a part of Chelsea life at this time.

   The temptation of sweets was something that was very difficult to avoid, for there were three sweet shops, or to give them their proper name, Newsagents, in the Worlds End alone, and like most of the other shops at this time they were all family-owned and run businesses. One of these was a shop called Fields, which was on the King Road opposite Slaidburn Street. Inside you would find the owners, Mr and Mrs Tobias, a small and typically old-fashioned Jewish couple who always wore dark clothes, and they were often helped by their two sons, Tony and Michael. Tony would continue in the family tradition with his own shop, Mr Tobias' Sweetshop, which was just a little way along the Kings Road. The other two shops were around the corner in Limerston Street: Fairmans, a family business again, which was run by Mr and Mrs Fairman along with their son Raymond (who some years later, after marrying my sister Pauline, was to become my brother-in law), and a few doors along was Andys, which was run by the solitary Andy herself. As if that wasn't enough, there were a further three within a quarter of a mile, two of which, Penningtons and Bizzies, we kids would have to pass on our way to school. Of course they were all crammed to the gills with shelves of large, glass jars filled to the brim with their multi-coloured and many-shaped alluring sweeties. Bizzies was known locally as 'Swizzies', for in those days sweets were sold by weight, usually a few ounces at a time. They would be weighed out on the shop scales and poured into a paper bag to be presented to the eagerly awaiting urchin. Sometimes the shopkeeper was given the choice of supplying slightly less or slightly more of the chosen sweets, and most of them, being of a generous nature, would always opt for the latter, but, alas, not Mr Bizzie, who, just like in The Beatles song 'Mean Mr Mustard', really was such a mean old man, for he would always make sure that the scales were tipped in his favour.

Of course, sweets were a year-round temptation, but the shops were also supplied for a short time once a year with something far more alluring: these were fireworks, and their explosive arrival was much anticipated. Come October all of us would, on a daily basis, pester the local shopkeepers: 'Any fireworks yet mister?'. We must have driven them mad, and I'm sure we helped to bring forward their arrival, if only to give them some peace ... but one thing was for sure, it would be the end of the peace for nearly everyone else.

BONFIRE NIGHT

This brings us to one of the most important events of the year for us Chelsea kids, and no, it wasn't Christmas - it was, of course, Bonfire Night - which was by far the biggest night of the year in most of the streets around the Worlds End. Preparation for the big event would start weeks before November 5, with all the different local gangs competing to gather their own stockpiles of wood etc. for the essential street fire. Bonfires had been even more important back in Cyril's childhood for as people were then so poor, the fire would have been the main, if not the only attraction. For fireworks required money and would therefore have been very scarce; but, apart from that, things were pretty much the same.

In preparation for the big night a game of wits would ensue between all of us cunning street urchins and the dreaded council men. London has never been short of waste so there were always things to burn, and in the sixties with its many bomb-sites and derelict houses it would offer us a plentiful supply of material for the fire; our only problem being to keep it all hidden until the big night. Inevitably, some of the stashes were discovered, and the accursed council men would load it all into an open-back truck and remove it to the dump, but, as I said, we were very cunning, and would always make sure that we had more than one stash hidden away. We were most industrious, and all of our wood-gathering had to be carried out at weekends or after school, taking us into the early evening, which being winter and by this time dark made our chances of not getting caught considerably better.

At the same time most of the younger kids would also roam the streets collecting money by requesting a penny for the guy. The guy was made from scrounged clothes: trousers, jumpers and any other bits and bobs we could find. These were then stuffed with paper, onto which a crude head was attached; the thing was then put in a cart and pushed around the streets. The best ports-of-call were most certainly the pubs, and with these the timing was everything. If you got your timing just right, which meant that the men would have had a few drinks and that no one else had been there before you, quite a haul could be got from their boozy inhabitants. Everyone on the streets was hailed or pestered by these little groups of beggars, with their familiar pleading cry of: 'Penny for the guy mister or misses!' The money made was spent almost entirely on the buying of fireworks, bangers were the most popular, and many fights would be had between rival street gangs who, as part of their entertainment, would light them and then throw them at each other. They cost two pence each or three pence for the fat ones, and over the two to three weeks before Bonfire Night we would get through quite a lot of them, as we also set about blowing up many bottles, or even putting them through the letter-boxes of the more unpopular grown-ups in the area.

On the big night the first thing that had to be done was the building of the bonfire. A continuous shuttle of kids of all ages would ferry the jumbled collection of wood, lino and anything else that would burn, from its hiding place and into the street, and in what seemed no time at all a large bonfire would appear. Finally, the unfortunate Guy, his work now done, would be placed on top, and the fire was hurriedly lit before it was discovered ... and away it all went. Considering that this was a residential street one would imagine the fire to be reasonably sized, but this was never the case, as with us size was everything, and we would build a pyre of anything up to fifteen feet high. One particular year, I think it was 1966, the fire burned so high and strong that it burnt through the telephone cables strung across the street from the tops of the houses. Now, when you think that the cables were around 40 feet high, is it any wonder that the heat given off was so intense that it also cracked some of the glass in the windows of those houses closest to it - all much to the anger of their residents.

With the fire now ablaze the serious business of letting off all the fireworks could now begin. Every family would be out on the street having their own firework display, and one by one, Roman Candles, Whizzbangs, Jumping Jacks, Rockets or Catherine Wheels, were let off. Now Cyril, being one of the better-off in the street, and certainly the most generous, guaranteed that we always had the biggest collection. Most of the kids would crowd around outside our house in anticipation of the fireworks that old money-bags Devenport had got this year, and, as ever, would all benefit from Cyril's generosity, as one by one the biggest fireworks of the night were let off by him.

As the evening progressed things would get pretty dangerous, and it would become more and more of a challenge to do all the things with the fireworks that you were not supposed to do. Many of us would hold Roman Candles or Flashbangs and fire them around the street. Rockets were placed in bottles, which were sometimes propped just off horizontal, so that they could be shot along the length of the street. Opposing sides would form from the many people there, and a kind of mock warfare would be played out, with bangers being thrown, and all sorts of things fired back and forth, with even the grown-ups joining in. Incredibly, over the many years of these dangerous, but thrilling, Bonfire Nights, there was only one bad accident. This happened when one of my friends who, like most of us, had a pocket full of bangers, was unlucky enough for them to catch alight, and as a result he suffered terrible burns.

Eventually the fire brigade would arrive, and accompanied by the boos and the jeers of the whole street they would reel out the hoses from their huge old fire-engine, and in no time at all put out our fire. This was just another exciting part of the evening's entertainment - our own private performance right on our doorsteps of the Chelsea Fire Brigade. No sooner had they left to race off to yet another street for yet another performance than we would all set about the building of the next fire, and the whole process would repeat again at some unknown time later that night. Eventually all the fireworks had been let off, the fire would burn down, and everyone would go indoors, leaving the street once again quiet, and the smouldering fire left all alone. Off we went to bed, smelling wonderfully of smoke and fireworks, to look forward to inspecting the inevitable damage done to the tarmac of the road the following morning.

Although Bonfire Night itself was over its energy was not quite spent yet, for it was always followed by the inevitable visit of the council surveyor who would come to inspect the pit burnt into the road by our fire, and arrange for its repair - something that had to be done every year. This was then followed by the arrival of a team of tarmac layers who, along with all of their machinery, which would include a huge steam-roller, would set up camp at the top of our street. There, a night-watchman would stay in a canvas hut, outside which a coke-filled brazier about the size of an oil drum would burn, its fire keeping him warm through the cold winter nights. His job was to guard all the equipment, but especially the large trailer full of potentially free coke that was required to fuel the steam roller. This was most tempting for many a Worlds End boy, and all sorts of distracting ploys would be used to get our hands on the black stuff during the few weeks that they worked around our streets. Invariably the night-watchman would be quite elderly, and would benefit from his position outside The Weatherby Arms by being brought drinks by Cyril and many of his friends. If he was friendly, as most of them were, we would take him bags of chestnuts; they were very popular at this time and were always cooked at home upon small shovels over our coal fires, but with the night watchman they would be placed upon a massive shovel to be cooked over the brazier. When they were nicely browned the challenge of removing the charred skin would begin; this would always result in some slightly burned fingers as we rushed to get at the sweet, smoky-tasting, brain-shaped nut inside. So there we all sat, munching away, avidly listening as he told us stories, which, like so many of the older generation of the time, would inevitably revolve around the war. We would try to persuade him, sometimes successfully, to be allowed upon the massive steam-roller, for these huge machines were a source of endless wonder for us London kids, most of whom had never even seen a tractor. These usually nice old men, were only too glad to have any kind of company through the long nights ahead, so we often got our way, and would scramble all over the huge, sleeping giant that was in our midst. When they left, the street would have a nice new square of tarmac where the fire had been, resembling a new rug, and also, more importantly, serving as a marker for the bonfire at next year's Bonfire Night.

Sometime at the end of the 1960s we were to have, even though we did not realise it at the time, our last bonfire in the street, and, indeed, our last proper Bonfire Night.

ALL THE FUN OF THE FAIR

Easter was a time that us Worlds End kids looked forward to with great excitement, for it not only meant that we would have a break from school, but more importantly, it signalled the opening of what at the time was the biggest Fun Fair in Britain. Battersea Fun Fair was situated in The Festival Gardens which were inside Battersea Park, and, conveniently for us, a mere half a mile from the Worlds End. The park held many attractions: there was a tree walk, a grotto, and a lake in which we could fish or, even better, hire wooden boats to row around on warm summer days. But all these would become redundant with the arrival of the fair. Battersea Fun Fair was, like so much else in Britain at this time, a collection of family-owned businesses, many of which were run by proud gypsy families. Their space in the fair was rented for the season, and with a healthy competition they would all set out to outdo each other with great gusto; this was something that the gypsy people, as can be witnessed even today with their fantasy-style weddings, were just brilliant at. Add to this the costumed collection of Teddy Boys who, along with the Mods and Rockers, gave the place a slightly dangerous edge, add the music, and the scene was set for the great theatre that was the Fun Fair.

Easter Sunday marked the big day, and would begin with the Easter Parade which ran through the park along the road which connected the entrances from either Chelsea Bridge or Albert Bridge. The Parade was made up of a collection of motorised floats all carrying a cast of characters: musical, historical or hysterical. It was good fun, but was just the prelude to the real business of the day which, with its conclusion, would signal the opening of the fair. You joined the queue and eventually reached the old-fashioned turn-stiles. Kids paid six pence and the adults one shilling. The turn-stile clunked, and then there you were in a whole other world, the smell of candy floss and hot dogs mixing with the multitude of blaring music and flashing lights filling the air - we were in heaven.

   The first sight to greet the eyes was the Sky Rocket Ride: two-seater sci-fi rockets painted in garish colours and covered in chromium bands. The Rocket Ships were attached to long steel arms, enabling you to steer them up and down as they rotated around, giving you a birds-eye view of all the attractions to come. Almost opposite was a line of side-shows, the favourite by far being called 'Knock the Lady out of Bed'. Raised on a platform was a single bed containing a pretty girl, dressed in a skimpy nightdress. Below her stood a small target with a button as a bullseye at its centre. For six pence you would purchase three wooden balls with which you would attempt to hit the small button, thereby scoring a bullseye. When this happened bells rang and lights flashed, attracting people from all around, who would race forward to witness the knocking of the lady out of bed. The bed would tip, and out she would roll, skipping and frolicking around in her naughty nightie for a few tantalising seconds to the cheers of the crowd, before returning - now to the jeers of the crowd - all too quickly back to the warmth and safety of her covers,. She would then pick up her newspaper, settle herself down, and wait for some lucky punter to again strike the bullseye which set the whole process off once again.

   Two of the favourite rides, especially with boys and girls of a certain age, were the Caterpillar, and, of course, the Ghost Train, both of which gave cover and subdued light, which would allow one to have a little kiss and cuddle if your luck happened to be in. The Caterpillar was comprised of a circle of open carriages which ran around on an undulating track. It would gradually build up speed, and upon reaching top speed a canvas canopy, painted like the skin of a caterpillar, would slowly close over the whole thing, giving it the appearance after which it was named. At this point it would also issue strange sounds, none of which had the slightest thing to do with caterpillars, but their reason becoming clear as it slowed, and the roof was raised once more to reveal most of the couples looking a little dishevelled, and some red in the face - wonderful, simple fun. More of the same would occur inside the Ghost Train, which being a longer ride and having a slightly spooky element, would allow for even more disarray to the clothing and hair of some of the lucky punters. You would be amazed at the places that lipstick can get in such a short space of time in the dark.

There was the Water Chute, where long carriages were hauled to the top of the U-shaped track, which would then turn to speed down the other side in free-fall to hit the water below, sending a large wave up against the glass wall from where spectators would watch; they never failed to jump back as the wall of water crashed against the glass. The Dodgems or 'Hitems', as they should more accurately be named, were by far the most popular and also by some way, the noisiest ride at the fair. With the music blaring, the main intention of the drivers was to build up as much speed as possible, select their target, and hit them as hard as they could. They were always a favourite, and at the end of each ride a free-for-all would begin as people raced to grab their car before they were all gone. In those days they were beautifully made - solid, heavy, highly polished and dripping in chrome with their power supplied by a pole which connected to an electrified mesh which covered the ceiling. They moved quite fast, and when in collision at speed would give you quite a jolt leaving many a person with a well-earned but rather stiff neck. Sadly today, in what has become our Nanny State, compensation based culture this would probably be called 'whiplash', so would be deemed quite unacceptable. Thankfully we were made of sterner stuff back then and being such wonderful fun, the glorious Dodgems were something you just could never get enough of and so were well worth the small price of a pain in the neck. The largest ride in the fair was the Big Dipper. This at the time was the largest helter-skelter in Europe and ran almost the whole length of one side of the fairground. It was very popular, but always looked a bit dodgy to me, so this was one ride that I usually avoided. All of this cost money, and, again, I was blessed to have Cyril as my benefactor. Where most of my friends would be lucky to get a couple of shillings from their parents, Cyril would invariably give me a ten bob note, and sometimes even a pound. Consequently, this enabled the whole gang to have more fun at the fair, as the money would inevitably be shared amongst us - for there's no fun in a fair when you're on your own.

  Being with Cyril anywhere was always guaranteed to be entertaining, so it was no surprise when one day at the fair he would treat us all to a typical piece of Cyril theatre. Occasionally the whole family would go together to the fair, and on this particular day I, along with my sisters, pressured Cyril to have a go on the Rotor. The Rotor was a huge spinning drum, inside which up to twenty people would stand with their backs to the wall. The drum would then revolve, building up speed, and gradually the floor would descend, leaving the occupants pinned to the wall by centrifugal force. The spinning would also create an up draught, as many unfortunate girls would find out, as they struggled to pull their skirts or dresses down from over their heads. This was all great fun to watch, but being inside was quite unpleasant and something none of us youngsters were willing to do. The audience sat around and above the drum in order to watch the spectacle. Having persuaded Cyril to have a go, off he went, game as always. Round went the drum and round went Cyril. As the rotor built up speed it became clear to all of us that Cyril's trousers, which were heavily weighed down with all the coins required for a father of five at the fun fair, were succumbing to the weight, and were now slowly descending. The force of gravity was overcoming the centrifugal force which kept the powerless Cyril, except for his trousers, pinned firmly to the wall. With each pass the weight of the coins dragged his trousers ever lower, which was greeted with shrieks of laughter from the whole crowd. Down went the floor, and all the way down went Cyril's trousers along with it, and there he was, our father, spinning around pinned to the wall, his trousers around his ankles, resplendent in his baggy, white underpants (which fortunately stayed put) for the whole crowd to see. The floor began to rise and the Rotor slowed to a stop, leaving all of the participants reeling around dizzily, trying to regain their senses. Amongst them was Cyril, stumbling about heaving up his trousers, while at the same time bending to collect the culprits of the piece which, of course, were all of the coins which had naturally fallen from his pockets and now littered the whole of the wooden floor. He thought it was all great fun, as did we, though I must say my mother could not resist the chance of stating: 'Trust you to show us up!' It was the perfect finale, and we all laughed our way out of the park across Albert Bridge and the ever present Father Thames, and all the way home to the Worlds End.

By the mid-1970s the Fun Fair had become a little jaded, its gaudy, noisy Sci-Fi feel, so perfect for the 50s and 60s, was not working its magic in the same way any longer. The struggle to survive would not be helped by the fatal accident involving the Big Dipper in 1972, which was to cost five people their lives. Its day was done, and the fun had all been spent ... so in 1974 it was to close its gates for the last time.

FOOTBALL CRAZY

To say that football was important to us would be something of an understatement, for it permeated the lives of almost everyone in the 50s and 60s, young and old alike. Looking back it's hard to believe that we had the time to do anything else, for it seems that all of our time was spent either kicking a ball in the streets (much to the irritation of some of the neighbours for broken windows were inevitable), in the park, or in the school playground, and when we weren't doing any of these we would be at Stamford Bridge watching Chelsea kicking, and getting kicked, in their attempts to play what was then more 'the Bootyfall Game' (in went the booty and down they'd fall), than 'the Beautiful Game'.

Every team had its hard-man, and Chelsea was no exception, being captained at the time by the appropriately named Chopper Harris. But no team ever reached the heights of brutality as that achieved by Don (note the Mafia link) Revie, with his trio of henchmen, Bremner, Giles and Hunter.

Cyril took me to my first match at Stamford Bridge when I was a mere five years old, and this would be followed over the coming years with many visits to various football grounds all over England, this would involve travelling long distances, many times by glorious steam trains. The men would set themselves up in the buffet car to be close to the booze, but it would also enable them to play cards at the tables there, and this would go on all the way to our destination. There would be a small interlude to see the match, and in no time at all we would be back on the train, with the men resuming the serious business of boozing and gambling all the way home - though it must be said that they always made sure that we kids were kept well supplied with our own choice of drinks, crisps and sweets.

Thanks to football and to Cyril, I was able to see much of the old, industrialised world that was England at this time, and upon many of these trips we would be accompanied by my eldest sister Pauline, who was, and still is, just a little football mad. Factories seemed to be everywhere, even lining the banks of the Thames through Chelsea, for in those days we really did manage to make a thing or two in this old country of ours, and the working-classes were the heart through which the life-blood flowed to make the whole thing work.

Football was a real working-class game back then and would be watched by whole families, my own being no exception. A typical Saturday would involve the arrival of uncles and cousins at Slaidburn Street for a sandwich and a cup of tea, before we all set off to join the stream of bodies passing through the Worlds End on their way to Stamford Bridge. Cyril would be accompanied by my mother Joyce, along with myself, my best mate Bone, his big brother Terry, any number of my four sisters, my Uncle Bill, cousin Charlie, and last but not least, Uncle Jim, making up our motley crew.

Strange things happen to some people at football matches, and this was the case with Uncle Jim. This private and quiet man would literally transform when it came to football; it was akin to Jeckyl and Hyde, for no sooner had the whistle blown than furious rants and rages would pour forth from his mouth, many of which could be quite obscene. This would eventually lead to my mother making sure that we all sat a good distance away from him to avoid any suspicion that he was one of us. After the match we would all troop back to Slaidburn Street where, with Uncle Jim restored to his former self, we would all sit down for a slap-up meal made by my mother and the girls.

Football in those days was always played on Saturday and the kick-off was at three o'clock all over the country, the only exceptions being cup replays or European matches, which were usually played on Wednesday nights. The grounds were mostly open terraces where the majority of fans would stand, making their capacity much higher than the all-seater stadiums of today, and crowds of 60,000 were not unusual.

On such days the streets of the Worlds End would come alive with the distant roar of the multitudes gathered to watch their teams battle it out in all weathers, and by the distinctive sounds they made it was possible to get a good idea of what was going on in the match. Of course, the loudest roar would always come when Chelsea scored, but it was also possible to identify a near miss, which came across the air as a collective sigh of disappointment, a corner, which was the unmistakable 'cooornerrr', or the wrong doing of an opposition player, or indeed the Referee, which would result in a loud gasp, followed by the inevitable 'boooh!'.

All these sounds grew much louder the closer you were to the stadium, and on a few occasions when not at the match I would specially visit the adjoining Brompton Cemetery. Brompton is one of London's great Victorian cemeteries - a magical place, which is only separated from Stamford Bridge by the railway line. The great roar of life coming from the match would wash over the endless rows of the assembled dead and their monuments, the sound falling and rising like an invisible choir, almost restoring to them their voices to create a quite remarkable bond between the past and the present ... an eerie but unforgettable experience.

Back on the streets, between the inevitable games of football which would carry on throughout the year, we also found time to play the more seasonable sports of tennis and cricket. Tennis was short-lived in our attention and would only be played during the few short weeks of June when Wimbledon was in progress, not too many miles away. The net would be built across the road using anything that we could get our hands on: chairs, boxes, clothes and any other inanimate object that happened to be lying around - though we did draw the line at using very old people.

The beginning of the Test Match season always resulted in the inevitable summer of street-cricket, which would be played using a tennis ball and wooden fruit-boxes as wickets. At times it seemed like the whole street was involved, with kids of all ages, both boys and girls, and even a few grown-ups joining in. All of this was accompanied by the glorious sound of the real thing pouring out onto the streets through the many opened windows from all the radios and televisions. Most sport was televised and in those days, all of our national sports were shown for the cost of the annual licence fee. You could really tell that it was summer, as these sounds accompanied you wherever you went right across the city.

Sadly, this is no longer the case in good old Britain, for not only has cricket been stolen from the people, but much international football has succumbed to the same spreading virus that is Sky television which, if only it could show a little grace and consideration, would realise that national sport belongs to the nation and is not just there to be SKYJACKED for those who can afford it, or, as is the case with many of our senior citizens, the ability or desire to even use a Skybox. It must, however, be said, that some responsibility also rests with the governing bodies, the clubs, and last but not least, the players themselves, who are all complicit in what has become the Sky-infested corporately-controlled money-pots that are now our national sports,

Chelsea returned to Wembley for their second F.A.Cup Final in 1970 (having lost their first to Spurs in 1967), this time to face THE DON Revie and his team of henchmen, otherwise known as Leeds United. Once again, just like in '67, the ball was set rolling for the complete redecoration of Slaidburn Street and much of the Worlds End. Windows were covered with photographs, rosettes and a myriad of blue and white regalia, while whole families worked together, constructing huge banners which stretched across the street saying: 'WIN OR LOSE UP THE BLUES' or, as was the case with our own: 'SEXTONS SIZZLERS' (Dave Sexton was Chelsea's manager). To round it all off, I spent many hours painting all the curb stones in the street with, you guessed it, blue and white paint, which was provided by Cyril. Some of this you can still see if you look closely, visible after more than forty years. They don't make paint like that anymore.

This was all just the prelude for the big day itself, which began with the gathering of all the Chelsea boys, and some girls, on the traffic island at the heart of the Old Worlds End. There we had time to inspect our costumes which included Bowler and Top Hats, painted appropriately, capes, suits, walking sticks, pyjamas, wigs and any number of personal adornments, all of course in good old

Chelsea blue. By now there was a real carnival atmosphere as we all larked about waiting for our transport which, appropriately, was a large open-back beer lorry, complete with a good supply of the aforementioned beer itself which, unlike us, did not have a return ticket. We left the Worlds End with all its decorations, which included the now demolished St John's Church, its roof newly emblazoned with the words 'Chelsea F.C.' This would get the aspiring artist, a Chelsea boy called Robert H., a bit of attention from the other boys in blue, and off we set for the journey across west London to the famous twin towers of the old Wembley Stadium. 'Bring on the DON'!

After a gruelling match, which finished with the scores even at 2-2, remaining undecided even after extra time, we set off on the back of the beer lorry feeling quite exhausted and just a little hoarse in the throat, to return to the Worlds End to celebrate. Of course, we hadn't actually won the Cup but we hadn't lost it either, and Worlds Enders never really needed an excuse to go out on the streets and get rowdy - and there was also the impending repeat performance of the replay to look forward to, or as it was known: 'BRING ON THE DON 2'.

The replay took place more than two weeks later; it was played on a Wednesday night and required us to make the long coach journey north to Manchester. This time THE DON and his boys got their just dessert as, after yet another brutal match, Chelsea went on to win 2-1, with the winning goal scored by the King of Stamford Bridge himself Peter Osgood, once again, in extra time. All of us Chelsea boys, after giving our all, were, yet again so hoarse and exhausted, that the journey back was spent in almost complete silence as we slept away the long miles home. The final act of the saga was played out the following Sunday morning when the Chelsea team, with their hard won trophy, paraded it from an open-top double-decker bus down the length of the Kings Road. Upon reaching the Worlds End, the beating heart of old Chelsea, the procession came to a grinding halt, stopped in its tracks by the sheer number of people who had turned out to welcome home their heroes; for just as it should be with proper heroes, they were all considered one of us, and as such would often be seen around Chelsea in the shops or, as was more likely, in any one of the numerous and thriving pubs that spread all along the

Kings Road at that time. When it was all over they would then return back to their everyday jobs as footballers.

Meanwhile, back on the streets life returned to normal, as we went about entertaining ourselves with the many street games that brought so much fun to us, but more than a little annoyance to the grown-ups. Knock down Ginger, Conkers, Tin Can Alley, hopscotch, British Bulldog, skipping, cards and Penny-up-the-Wall, were just some of the games that were played in between the inevitable game of football. Looking back, I find it hard to believe that there was time to fit them all in. Maybe it says something about the value of time spent in actual reality. Is it possible that there really was more time then! Or does it say something not only about the pace of modern life but the huge amount of time that so many of us, particularly the young, spend in virtual reality, for it seems to me that, wonderful as computers are, they also seem to be able to suck out our time, which all just disappears as if down a black hole, its appetite never satisfied. The greatest loss in the relentless march of the virtual world must be the shared joy that was once common on all the streets of our land, and the valuable life experience gained from using your ingenuity along with your friends to create your own fun. As we retreat further and further into our virtual shells I can only wonder if the accepted image of the grey-skinned alien with his huge head, oversized eyes, emaciated body and spider-like fingers, is the fate that awaits us all unless we learn to place a greater value upon our Actual Reality. Maybe the time has come for us all to make a reality check and return just like E.T. - HOME.

Having won the F.A.Cup the previous year, 1971 saw Chelsea travel around Europe in pursuit of the Cup Winners Cup. The quarter final was a two-leg affair which involved the Devenport clan travelling to the old medieval city of Bruges in Belgium. After a bus ride from the airport we all set off for what turned out to be a long hike to the ground, this proved to be a real challenge for Cyril who had suffered from back trouble for some years and this had now reached the stage of creating loss of feeling in his legs, so along the way we stopped for a much needed beer or two in a Flemish bar. One thing was immediately obvious - we were no longer in swinging London, and much of the city, including the people, were still almost medieval, and I, with my long hair, would bring us close to the edge of not reaching the match at all. The bar was packed mostly with Bruges fans who took great delight practising their limited grasp of English upon me: 'Is 'im boy or is 'im girl?' raised a few laughs the first time it was uttered, but after a few beers the novelty had most definitely worn a bit thin. One particularly oafish looking Flemm approached me and uttered once again: 'Is 'im boy or is 'im girl?' I had by now had quite enough, and just as I was about to take a swing at him, my rather more astute brother-in-law, Ray, wrapped his arms around me from behind, pinning my arms to my side. His timely intervention, had without a doubt, saved us all from a beating on what would have definitely been, a badly losing wicket.

Chelsea progressed all the way to the Final, which would take us all even further afield to Athens in Greece at the beginning of May. Once again, my long hair turned out to be quite a focal point, and along with my similarly adorned friend Tony S., we would become the objects of much fascination to many of the Greeks, or as they were affectionately known to us: 'The Bubbles' (Bubble and Squeak, Greek). The Bubbles would hang out of windows as the two blond bombshells passed, or come pouring out of shops and bars to gawp at us as if we had just landed from another planet - but hey, the Kings Road was like another planet compared to most places, so maybe they had a point.

As was now becoming a habit, Chelsea again drew in the Final ,the score, 1-1 after extra time, and the replay was arranged for the following Tuesday. Fortunately for us, Cyril had booked us in for the week; sadly, some of the fans had only been able to come for the weekend, and as a consequence were to miss being at the replay and would have to settle for watching it, along with many others (unfortunately for me as I would soon find out), on their black and white TVs back home. Chelsea eventually went on to beat Real Madrid 2-1, and when the final whistle blew the two blond bombshells vaulted the wire fencing surrounding the pitch, avoiding the armed troops who, being in Greece which was governed by a military junta, acted as security guards. We reached the players and for a few short moments joined in the frenzy of celebration before being unceremoniously restored to the terraces, all portrayed beautifully for the TV cameras.

Upon my return to London, and more importantly, to school, I proceeded to my form room armed with the then required sick-note, to explain my absence for the past week. My form master took great joy in receiving the said sick-note from the far from sick-looking, suntanned boy on display in front of all his classmates. He read it, had a good laugh, and the whole class cheered, for as I found out, my face had been gloriously displayed for everyone to see on the good old BBC.

1971 would turn out to be a year of 'finals' for me. It would be my final year at school, which meant I could join my sister Sue, who at this time worked for Cyril, alongside his many workmen. It would be my final year as a Chelsea boy, as rapid changes in my life would send me spinning off in a quite different direction, and it would also be my final year as an attending Chelsea fan, as the appeal of hairy legs in shorts on Saturday afternoons was replaced by the far more tantalising attraction of the shapely legs in mini-skirts that were abundantly displayed at the same time along the Kings Road.

With my school years over and now being at work full-time this would give Cyril the opportunity to deal with his increasingly bad back, and so, after much consultation, he went into the Royal Masonic Hospital for a laminectomy which is an operation to fuse parts of the spine. It turned out that some twenty years before Cyril, who was in Liverpool for a football match, had been the victim of mistaken identity and had been badly beaten by Chelsea fans which had resulted in his spine being fractured. This had not been found at the time and so over the years his spine having set badly was to cause him much pain. This procedure was not without its risks for he had been warned that there was a possibility of paralysis to his legs, and even if successful he would have to wear an orthopaedic corset for the rest of his life - but he had little choice. The operation turned out to be a great success and Cyril was soon up to his old tricks in the hospital ward with his bedside cabinet stocked to the rafters with whisky, gin and beer, all of which he dispensed with great gusto, making him the life and soul of the place. As for the corset - he hated it, and struggled with it for about a month, and then one day just threw it aside and that was that.

CHAPTER SIX

The Best Room

*An idea, like a ghost,
must be spoken to a little
before it will explain itself.*
-Charles Dickens.

The best room was an odd feature of some working class London homes, being a place set aside for use only on special occasions. Ours was up two flights of stairs on the first-floor of our crowded, Victorian town-house. It contained a three-piece-suite, a low wrought-iron glass-top table, a wonderful old HMV radiogram with a hydraulic lid, and our pride and joy - the cocktail cabinet, filled to bursting with glasses, many bottles of strange coloured liqueurs, and, of course, spirits. It also happened to be the largest room in the house, but was rather strangely the least used, the family choosing to cram into the much smaller front room directly below it on the ground floor, which meant that it would only come to life on special occasions like Christmas, parties or upon the death of a close family member.

The best room, though empty of human occupants for much of the time, was never completely unoccupied, for it also had a life of its own. There was always a strange atmosphere in the room, and you would often feel compelled to look over your shoulder in anticipation of finding someone there, but, of course, there was nothing to be seen, there would just be the usual strong and very other-worldly presence. Many times, when in our favoured room down below, we would hear footsteps passing above our heads, making the boards creak as they passed at a gentle pace from one side of the room to the other. So, as you can see, it was very hard to feel that you were ever really alone in the best room, and you probably never were, for over the years a number of unforgettable incidents would occur there.

One winter night (it must have been Christmas), the family were all gathered in the best room, playing what had as usual turned into a raucous game of cards when, all of a sudden, out of nowhere, came the most deafening crack, which I can only describe as sounding just like a pistol shot. We were stopped dead in our tracks, and the room fell silent, until out of the silence came the voice of my mother. 'What on earth was that?', she remarked . None of us had the slightest idea, and after a little investigating had failed to provide any obvious answers we went back to the card game. The following day, my mother, whilst returning some glasses to the cocktail cabinet, happened to brush against one of the set of her six much treasured cut-crystal glasses, which were rarely used but always kept there. The top of the glass, that she had barely touched, fell away about half an inch down, and on closer inspection it appeared as if it had been sliced cleanly through with a knife. My mother immediately went to the remaining five which stood, seemingly in one piece, all in a line. One by one she removed them, to find to her horror that an identical cut had been made through each and every one, the break only becoming evident when they were moved, and the two pieces came apart. There was no obvious explanation for what had caused this strange event and we never did work it out, but all being quite used to odd happenings in our home it was just put down to yet another oddity of the best room.

    Another incident involved my sister Sue. Sue is not someone who could be said to have a nervous nature, and even at the age of fifteen when this incident occurred, was not easily scared. She was and still remains, a very tough cookie. One day, while alone in the room, Sue was stood looking out through the window onto the street below, when suddenly she felt the air chill all around her. She then noticed, reflected in the glass and seemingly standing right behind her, a strange man wearing a dark suit and a bowler hat. Not recognising him she turned in alarm, only to find empty space, for there was no one there. She screamed, raced from the room, and quite understandably gave it a wide berth for some time after.

    The best room would finally become a bedroom for the last few months of our mother's life. After being put through the mill with tests, scans and blood transfusions in her many visits to various hospitals, she was finally diagnosed with cancer of the pancreas, and given a maximum of six months to live. With this dreadful news it was unanimously decided that our mum would see out her days at home with all of us, her family, to be with her and care for her. Due to the constant visits of our good friend and family doctor, Paul Brass, along with the even more constant comings and goings of her large family, it was decided to move our mother from her small bedroom into the much bigger and lighter best room. These were to be some of the most difficult and painful days of our lives, but they would also be some of the most rewarding.

Throughout her illness she was never alone, being surrounded by her children and her many grandchildren who all adored her, and who would upon many occasions spend the night with her. In many ways her grandchildren were closer to her than to their own mothers, for being a gifted healer it was always to her that they would turn whenever they were in need, demanding to be taken to Nanny at all hours of the day or night. Her healing abilities were remarkable, and something that we all relied upon, and over the years we were all to witness and benefit from her special touch. She really made us all feel safe, for there didn't seem to be any fight that she could not win, as she applied her magic creams or concocted her own special medicines like Cyril's 'Jollop' for his smoker's cough. Her healing powers were used not only for people but with all our animals, and the many sick plants which friends would bring her – all of which thrived from her special touch. Unfortunately, her gift with which she had helped so many others would be something with which she could not help herself.

She was a brave person, but for some unknown reason our mother had always had a terrible fear of the dark, and this was something that throughout her illness we were all more than aware of. With this in mind I had made the strange request that one of us (her children), would be sleeping when she finally passed over, for I truly believe in a connection between the dream world and the spirit world. She fought like a tiger to eke out her precious days, but the end drew visibly closer, and eventually, with no fight left, she slipped into a coma. The whole family gathered for the vigil, which was to go on for a few days and nights, and upon one of these nights I decided to get some sleep in my mother's usual bedroom; a place in which I had not slept since I was a child. Sleep came immediately, and the next thing I knew I was being woken by one of my sisters to tell me that mum was going. I collected myself quite calmly, for inside I knew that she had already gone, and that I had been the one to be asleep during her final journey. I cannot say that I remember anything that happened during her passing, but remain convinced that I was allowed to accompany her in some way on her journey to the next world. She had left life just as she had lived life, surrounded by the enormous love of her close family who had been with her throughout her final ordeal.

The atmosphere in the room was incredibly strong as we all shared in what was not only a release for her, but for all of us as well. It had been an intense and exhausting six months, and my sisters had been magnificent - especially Carol, who in many ways is the most like mum of all of us.

During that long night another strange thing was to occur. Carol, with her hands already full, had also had to deal with a sickness that had affected her youngest child, my nephew Paul. Paul was around four at the time and had come down with a high fever. This had affected him rather strangely, as he claimed to be holding a heavy, silver ball which, of course, none of us could see. He repeatedly held out his hands in order to show it to us, asking Carol many times: 'What is it mum, why is it so heavy?' Naturally we were all concerned by this, and decided that he needed to see a doctor.

At 9 o'clock I set off with Carol and Paul to see our by now very familiar family doctor, Paul Brass. Dr Brass was most upset by the death of our mother who, as he told us, had been not only a patient but a good friend for many years. He had respected her enormously, and praised the great courage she had shown throughout her ordeal. While he examined Paul I sat in the waiting room along with his secretary Helen. As anyone who has lost someone so close will know, things are not quite normal in these circumstances, and as I sat there memories of all the times that I had made this very journey as a boy along with my mother, passed through my mind just like a movie.

In those days the busy reception was run by an efficient and formidable lady called Nelly, who would pull your records from the vast array of wooden drawers that covered the wall behind her counter. Nelly was really the first line of defence for the three doctors who made up the surgery, and she wasted no time in showing malingerers and time-wasters her disapproval - but she was always friendly to all of us, I'm glad to say. Now, armed with the required records, we would sit to wait our turn along with all the other coughing and sneezing patients. After his usual warm greeting Dr Brass would turn to my mother and ask her for her diagnoses, and as was always the case he would congratulate her upon her answer, for as he said himself, 'There's not much I can tell you Mrs Devenport.' Returning to the present I sat pondering how we as a family could ever thank him for the enormous amount of time and very personal care he had given to our mother. I called to Helen who was sat across the room behind her desk, and asked her if Dr Paul had any hobbies or was a collector of any kind. She thought for a moment, and then replied, 'I believe he collects those small Japanese ivory figures. Oh! What are they called?' As soon as she had posed the question I heard my mother's voice clearly state: 'Netsuke'.

I then passed the answer to Helen who replied, 'That's it, I can never remember what they are called.'... Well, neither could I, but mum obviously could. Coincidentally, I had bought my mother two such figures some years previously whilst in Hong Kong, and now, with her blessing, we were to pass them on as a small thank you from our family to Dr Brass. He was very touched by this, the more so because they had belonged to her. Carol now returned, greatly relieved, as Dr Brass after a thorough examination could find nothing wrong with Paul, and could only put his symptoms and hallucinations down to some of the strange things that he had witnessed with the passing of one so close.

The best room was once again transformed to await the return of our mother from her short stay with the family undertaker, Jimmy Buckle, whose local family business had always taken care of the funerals of the Devenports, all the way back to my grandfather. Once again, the white sheets were hung over the windows, the cross and candlesticks borrowed from the church, the incense was lit, and our mother, whose coffin had been carefully manipulated up the narrow staircase, was placed amongst them, to then be surrounded by many flowers. Over the next few days we were all able to spend time with her; this would allow us in our own private way to say our goodbyes. It was really very special. Our mother however had one last act to carry out, and having died a few days previously it would be something that was quite inexplicable but very moving, and occurred whilst our father Cyril was saying his last goodbyes.

As he was talking to her a tear appeared in the corner of one of her eyes, and gently rolled down onto her rosy cheek. Cyril was shaken by this, and left the room, now in floods of tears of his own, to tell us what had happened. Along with my sisters we went to see for ourselves, and just as he had described, there was the tear upon her cheek for all to see. How this could be we will never know, but there are some things that you just have to accept, no matter how impossible they may seem. This was certainly one of them. God Bless you Mum.

The sheet was again sent around the street, and all of our neighbours contributed various amounts to make up the grand sum of £57, with which we bought a wreath to add to the great many flowers that mum received.

CHAPTER SEVEN

THE WONDERFUL MRS G

*Variety's the very spice of life,
That gives it all its flavour.*
-William Cowper.

Working with Cyril was never anything other than a sheer delight, for being the social animal that he surely was, work, just as with the rest of his life, was guaranteed to be one whole lot of fun; so, it should come as no surprise that I was to leave school at the young age of fifteen in order to join him on his interesting journey. The average day would start with us visiting his jobs in various parts of London which involved delivering materials, checking the progress of the work and having a chat with the clients and the men, with the usual cup of tea thrown in. This always included a few laughs, and would generally take us up to around midday. This part of our work now over, Cyril would then suggest dropping in upon whoever was the nearest of one of his many clients. Although they had not been forewarned his arrival was always welcomed, and before you knew it there he'd be, sat chatting with one or other of the many ladies that made up his varied clientele, and drinking the first of the day's many drinks; it was all as they say: 'just in a day's work'. He was a cherished friend to all of his clients who, it must be said, were mostly ladies - and this brings me around to one lady in particular, who was to figure very strongly throughout the rest of his working life - the wonderful Mrs G.

Mrs Garnett, or Mrs G, as she was affectionately known, really was a wonderful person. She was a striking woman, quite tall for the time, with sharp features and piercing blue eyes, always subtly but immaculately made up, and her clothes, although conservative, were carefully chosen and gave her a very smart appearance. Her hair, which she mostly wore up, was covered with a great variety of hats, and in the more than twenty years that I knew her she hardly changed at all. She spoke with a strong, highbrow accent, and many of her sentences were rounded off with a very high pitched 'Mmmm.' Having lost her one and only husband during the Second World War at the tender age of thirty-four she was never to remarry, choosing instead to devote her life to her work and her many friends who, if you were lucky enough to count yourself amongst them, you could count yourself very lucky indeed, for she had the most desirable of characteristics of integrity and generosity, added to which she was never anything other than herself. In this there were obvious similarities to Cyril, and when their paths crossed in the late 1950s it was to forge the beginnings of a very strong friendship and an equally strong working relationship, which was to last for the rest of her life. They say 'timing is everything', and for Mrs G and Cyril this would certainly prove to be the case.

Mrs G had just opened her first shop which she called simply, Home Decorating. It was situated in Walton Street at the heart of Chelsea; this was to be one of the first complete interior design shops in London, and it would require a good team of reputable builders and decorators to fulfil the many services which it was to provide … and Cyril was to be just the man for the job. To say that Mrs G was well connected would be something of an understatement, for how many people would be able to call upon their good friend the young Queen Elizabeth to preside over the grand opening of their shop. This was done as a personal favour by the Queen to Mrs G, and is probably something that would be quite unimaginable today.

The Home Dec, as we called it, was a most interesting place indeed for it was completely manned (excepting Stan who ran the stockroom and was therefore carefully hidden away), by women. On the top-floor were a collection of offices, the largest of which was occupied by Mrs G and her sister, Lilah. In the other various rooms could be found the secretaries and accountants, all mature ladies and all friends of Mrs G's, busily typing or book-keeping. The first- and ground-floors were the showrooms and these were staffed by an ever-changing collection of glamorous debutantes who, as we were to find out over the years, were themselves part of the Home Dec's many attractions, for Cyril was to attend many of their society weddings as the girls were gradually picked off by hot-blooded members of the upper classes.

Mrs G's right arm was her sister Lilah Fortescue. Lilah was a very private lady with none of the gregariousness of her sister, and at times could even be a little gruff, especially with men, and she made it quite clear that she really had little time for any of them. She always wore dark wool suits with the skirt hanging well below the knee, and a white lace blouse under the jacket. Her hair was always worn up with a bun at the back ... all in all very Edwardian.

I would often have to call upon Mrs G in her large office which was situated at the top of the building. Upon knocking at the door I would be greeted with the familiar 'come in!' from one or the other of the inseparable sisters. Upon entering, a furious white blur would race across the room, barking and growling, to attach itself to one of my feet; this was Scrappit, the formidable white and brown Yorkie, who had a particular bone to pick with anyone who was not of the fairer sex. I would then proceed to walk across the room with the growling Scrappit firmly attached to my foot, accompanied by Mrs G saying, 'Put him down Scrappit!' What fun!

One day, having gone to the Home Dec to collect Mrs G, Cyril and I entered the upstairs office as usual, there we encountered not only the angry Scrappit but an equally angry Lilah on what for her must have been a particularly bad day. She was most bad tempered and quite unnecessarily rude to us both, and so we left the shop with Mrs G, feeling rather awkward and embarrassed by the rudeness of her sister. Once inside the privacy of our car she turned to us and said, 'I really am most terribly sorry about that; Lilahs behaviour was quite uncalled for.' Mrs G was most discreet and never one to talk about anything personal, but on this one occasion she obviously felt that we deserved some kind of explanation, and so she went on to share something very private with us, which when told would explain the mystery of Lilah's strange ways over the many years that we had known her. She told us this remarkable story.

During the Second World War, Lilah, being young, very attractive, bright and fluent in a number of languages, had been trained as an agent, and was then sent into enemy-occupied France. Her particular mission would require her to infiltrate the occupying Nazi hierarchy, something this brave and intelligent young woman managed ably to accomplish, but which sadly would come at some personal cost. Something quite unforeseen was to follow, for the young Lilah had done her job rather too well, for having gained the trust of the Germans she was then to fall in love with one of their top-ranking officers. They say that all is fair in love and war, but it could not have seemed very fair to this young and attractive woman when, in her duty for King and country, she was forced to betray her lover, leading to his assassination and death. The very courageous Lilah, having lost this most unlikely, but what would turn out to be, the only love of her life, was to remain a spinster for the remainder of it. With the sharing of this very personal story Mrs G had guaranteed that the formidable Lilah, whatever her behaviour, would from now have only our full respect.

    She was to make up for the lack of a man in her life by surrounding herself with numerous dogs, all terriers of one kind or another (these breeds being her particular favourite), one of which was named Elvis ... even though he was not a hound dog he had a pretty cool name for the time.

    Once a year Mrs G would take a business trip to Paris; there she would visit many of the old wallpaper manufacturers that had existed in its back-streets for centuries. The purpose of her trip was to trawl through the stores of wood-blocks from which wallpapers were printed, and to select prints to add to the unique range which she had to offer in her London shop. Some of these designs had lain dormant for 100 years or more, and Mrs G would be responsible for their reintroduction into the decorating world.

    Through Mrs G we were to work in some of the most prestigious and beautiful houses in the land, which would include Buckingham Palace, St. James Palace, Kensington Palace and Windsor Castle, to name but a few, and we were to share many interesting times together as we set about redecorating some of the better parts of London. Loyalty was another quality that Mrs G shared with Cyril, and in the thirty years of their working relationship this was something that would never waver. She was by far the largest source of work throughout Cyril's career.

    On many occasions I would get to chauffeur the pair of them around London to inspect the work in progress on their many shared working projects. Mrs G would never fail to tell me, 'Oh Peter, you are the most wonderful driver. I feel so safe with you. Mmmm!' Personally, for me, it was a great relief to reach seventeen and pass my driving test, for being driven by Mrs G was a great test of ones nerve: she was a great lady, but, alas, no great driver.

Her tremendous energy was really quite remarkable; she had wonderful taste and an eagle-eye for detail. She would choose and supply all wallpapers, fabrics for the furniture and curtains, and oversee the making of the individual colours for the many paint surfaces, and even on occasion furnish entire houses right down to knives and forks ... all done with the greatest of ease, but, above all, with great taste.

The mixing of colours was always an interesting part of our work. A trestle table would be set up, which was then loaded with the many tubes of different paint-stainer required for the job. Mrs G would then produce the piece of fabric or wallpaper which contained the colour which Cyril, jacket off and shirtsleeves rolled up, would then set about matching. Cyril was an absolute natural with colour and would tear into the job with great gusto. He was, however, not the tidiest of workmen, and very soon the trestle table would be covered in splashes of paint, and with constant guidance from Mrs G: 'A splash more umber or ochre.' etc., he would perform his alchemical magic. The result was always as Mrs G put it, 'Perfect Cyril, you are such a good colour-maker. Mmmm.'

Almost all of Cyril's work would come through a number of lady interior designers, and in all his working years he ran his business on a recommendation-only basis; being in such demand he would never have the need to advertise. The lady designers would all vie for Cyril's sole attention and there was even a little jealousy between them, but Cyril, being a great ladies man (which was just as well having four daughters), would always manage to keep them all happy, and in his inimitable way make them all feel special. However, it must be said that his first priority was always Mrs G, for I know that to him she was always just a little more special.

Their working relationship blossomed and turned into the most creative partnership: Mrs G was always overflowing with ideas and Cyril, with his instinctive, natural ability, was more than able to bring her plans to fruition, and so over the years they would be great teachers to each other.

Together they set out upon a wonderful working journey which would take us around England, working in fine houses in the Cotswolds, Wiltshire, and to Mrs G's own home, the lovely Fairford Mill in Gloucestershire. This beautiful old mill-house had the waterwheel enclosed, and invariably I would stay with Cyril in the bedroom right above it. There we would be lulled to sleep by this incredibly powerful, but extremely gentle old-world machinery which had churned on endlessly through the centuries, utilising the clean energy of the passing river without creating the pollution which has become such a problem for us all in the present day.

Another journey which would take us even further afield would be our trip to Mrs G's ancestral home 'Castle Hill', Filleigh, North Devon, where we were to work for her uncle, Earl Fortescue, who had been one of the four canopy-holders in the Abbey at the coronation of the Queen. This was quite a journey from London, and would entail a whole team of men, which included Cyril's brother (my Uncle Pat), all of us boarding in the local pub in South Molton. The men especially enjoyed country work, which in this case was to keep them in Devon for six weeks. Cyril would make the long drive from London twice a week to inspect the work, but more importantly, always on a Friday to pay the men's wages. He would sometimes make the journey accompanied by Mrs G and myself. Mrs G would obviously stay at her family home whilst Cyril and I, much to my delight at the age of eleven years old, would stay at The Anchor pub with his team of men. After their day's work the men would spend the evening in the bar, drinking and playing cards or bar skittles. Being 1966 there was also the added entertainment of a small thing called The World Cup which, as we all know, was held in England that year, and I remember well sitting in the bar huddled round the small black and white TV with all the men. Most nights would finish with a sing-song, with my Uncle Pat playing the tunes on the pub's old piano. It was great.

Many years later, during the mid-80s, I returned to this pub, being on holiday in the area with a group of friends, including Simon Bere, also known as the Apprentice as he was new to our group, and

Ronnie Smith otherwise known as the Chancellor, for his approach to all things financial. Before leaving London I discussed my plan to revisit the pub with one of the original team of workmen who had stayed there. He asked me if I would enquire after a girl called Diane, who had worked there at the time as a barmaid, and I agreed to do just that. Arriving at the pub was very nostalgic, and even though many years had passed it had changed very little. I asked the landlord if he knew of Diane, the barmaid; he responded by telling me that it was a bit before his time, but then called across the bar to one of his customers who happened to be the son of the landlord during the 1960s. I was approached by a large, Devonish country man. We said, 'Hello', and I innocently repeated my question, asking him if he could remember a barmaid called Diane who had worked here in the 1960s. He looked back at me and replied in his thick accent, 'Whoy would thart be?' – so I told him about the men staying in the pub and that one of them had asked after her.

At this point his face turned quite black and he ranted angrily at me, 'That be moy wife yurr asking about, ee wurs err boyfriend weren't ee and ee gave her a ring!'

I had not quite bargained for this, for, after all, it was an awfully long time ago, but looking at the size and mood of him, and fearing for my neck I decided it was time to quit. I made my apologies and claimed I had been mistaken about the pub; we hurriedly left not only the pub but also the town, in our wake just a trail of dust. It was the kind of innocent faux pas that Cyril was so good at, and my friends had a great laugh at my expense - as did Cyril and all the workmen on my return to London.

During the late 1970s and early 80s the Home Dec was to expand considerably. The shop in Walton Street doubled in size and Mrs G was also to open a factory at Hartley Witney in Gloucestershire, where she now manufactured her own range of wallpapers and paints. Of course, we were engaged in transforming the London shop, during which a quite unique situation arose. We received a telephone call from one of our male clients who requested a meeting with Cyril, and it was arranged for him to visit us at home. His name was Tim, he was around forty and like most pukka chaps, was polite and well educated. One thing I will say for public school education is that it removes any sense of inhibition or shame, and gives those that receive it great versatility, not to mention abundant confidence. Tim did not beat about the bush; coming straight to the point he told us that he had been down on his luck a bit lately and was in a bit of a hole, and although he had no experience to offer, wondered if Cyril could employ him for a short time. This played into another of Cyril's great strengths for he was a natural benefactor, and I never knew him to refuse work to anyone; even upon the rare occasions when he had no work himself he would always find something for them to do. Of course, Tim was welcomed on board; Cyril told him to be with us on Monday whence he would furnish him with the required tools and overalls.

Tim, now suitably attired in white bib and braces, was put to work at Home Dec along with the five of us who were already working there. He was a great source of amusement to all the working-class chaps, who waited for him each morning to come swanning into work in his pinstripe suit, holding a briefcase containing his overalls. The men were a little bemused with him for a while, but soon, as Londoners do, took him under their wing to share many stories together over lunch and tea-breaks. During these breaks we would all seat ourselves around the room upon makeshift chairs, which would be a board suspended between two stepladders or an upturned bucket. Out would come the sandwich boxes or 'nosebags' as they were referred to, accompanied by the daily newspapers, which were invariably The Sun or The Mirror, but now, with the introduction of Tim to their ranks, the most unlikely sight of *The Times* would be added. One day, a chauffeur-driven Rolls Royce arrived outside the Home Dec out of which, to the amazement of us all, stepped the suited, briefcase-bearing Tim. Over tea that morning he informed us in his high-brow accent that the car belonged to an old bird he had met who had plenty of lolly, but unfortunately only one eye. He then went on to tell us that she had taken rather a shine to him, and using her mono-vision, and obviously liking what she saw, he had now become, literally, the apple of her one and only eye. He continued to work for us for just a few weeks after this, until one day he turned up at our home with his tools and brushes. He thanked Cyril for helping him, and then informed us that he was quite alright now as the old bird had died leaving him £30,000 and a cottage in Dorset. We never saw him again.

The now revamped Home Dec had brought about many changes to Mrs G's life, and the increase of responsibility and personnel was to create a great strain upon this hugely energetic lady. It would also, for the first time, bring men into the previously female domain of the Walton Street shop, some of whom, sadly, would take unfair advantage of her trust and generosity by pilfering contacts in order to set up their own businesses. The predatory instincts of certain kinds of men would play a large part in the failing of this once very genteel and successful business, and I know certainly added to the increasing bad health of Mrs G.

Having been unwell for some time she telephoned Cyril and asked if we would go and visit her in her lovely London home which was in Seymour Walk, Chelsea. I think we both knew that this was to be a special meeting, and off we went with a large bunch of roses as a gift to this most special English Rose. We were met at the door by Mrs G's very private sister, Lilah, who led us through this most familiar house, to pass on the way black and white photographs, in the style of, and probably taken by, Cecil Beaton himself, of both the sisters looking quite beautiful in their younger days. Finally reaching Mrs G's bedroom door we entered, and there was our great friend surrounded by all the furnishings of her immaculate taste and creativity in her private sanctum, and far from looking unwell she actually looked radiant, but she also looked quite as we had never seen her before. She was sat up in bed wearing a beautiful white linen nightdress, and for the first time in all of the years of our friendship, she was not only without make-up but was wearing her lovely long fair hair down, which fell gracefully onto her shoulders – again, a first. She asked us to sit either side of her on the bed, and doing just as we were told (for with Mrs G resistance surely was futile), we did just that, and each held one of her hands. We sat and listened as this great lady talked about all of the wonderful things we had done together and the great fun we had shared over the many years. She thanked us for being part of her life and for being such good friends. It was really most civilised, and as we both sat listening we came to realise that this great lady had brought us here in her own inimitable way to say 'Goodbye'. We kissed her upon her cheeks, and left, feeling extremely choked up, and once inside the privacy of our car both Cyril and I, now quite overcome with emotion, let it all out and had a good cry. It had been a most unusual morning, and an experience which I will always treasure, and one that summed up the enormous grace and courage of the wonderful Mrs G. God Bless her.

   With the passing of her elder sister and lifelong companion, Lilah, as you would expect, put on a brave face, but under her protective shell she was really and quite understandably devastated. The loss of someone so close in life obviously creates something of a void; but I believe that along with the loss there is always contained, if you care to accept it, also a gift. This was certainly the case with the once spiky and aloof Lilah, who was now to be transformed into a much softer person, and over the following years our relationship with her was to become closer, allowing us after all those years to become her good friends, and giving us the opportunity to visit her at home in Seymour Walk or at her lovely country home, a cottage called Angels, in the pretty village of Inkpen on the Berkshire, Wiltshire border. Our last time spent with Lilah would be at Angels: Cyril and I drove down from London to share what for me was a most memorable lunch, where for this one and only time Cyril, normally right at the heart of things, would take my usual place in the back-seat to become the listener, as I sat close to this most knowledgeable and interesting lady having a wonderful time discussing all things esoteric. She really was a fascinating person, and just as with her sister the wonderful Mrs G, we were most privileged to have known her and even more so to have been able to call her our friend.

CHAPTER EIGHT

THE FIRST STREAKER

As the tempo of the Swinging '60s in London began to increase the use of drugs by the young hip set was to draw not only the attention of the police, but the equally unwelcome attention of the British press. A series of articles ran in various newspapers focusing on our top educational institutions, and carried lurid stories about the drug-crazed goings-on of the students at Oxford and Cambridge. This caused quite a stir throughout the country as we were on the whole still a pretty staid lot, but even more so with the parents of the students, who also happened to be some of the wealthiest and most influential people in the land. Something just had to be done, so a number of the parents, in their typically eccentric and very British way, decided that the mysteries of marijuana deserved investigation, and as such would require much closer inspection. Who knows, maybe they thought that they themselves were missing out. After much discussion it was decided that a party would be held at the Chelsea home of a friend and client of my father's, the glamorous Lady Constance McIndoe, whose pretty house was, appropriately, just off the very swinging Kings Road.

Lady Mac, as we called her, was the widow of the brilliant pioneer of plastic surgery, Sir Archibald McIndoe, who through his groundbreaking work was to restore the dignity of so many of the brave young men who had suffered such terrible burns in the RAF during the Second World War. Over the many years that I knew her I was to meet some of these brave souls who, through her dedicated work with their appropriately named Guinea Pig Club, had become life-long friends, and would visit her at her Chelsea home. It was always very humbling and a great privilege to meet them.

Her Chelsea home was also used as a kind of hideaway, where many of her lady friends, not wishing to be seen at such a time, would convalesce after having their own nips and tucks. We were regular visitors to the home of Lady Mac, and so it was inevitable that upon occasion we would sometimes come across them. Although they easily recognised us, their identities after the surgery were not always immediately apparent, and we would have to tread very carefully so as not to cause any offence. These unfortunate ladies looked very sorry indeed, their faces, or the bits that could be seen, were covered in bruises and blown up like balloons from the effects of the surgery. They always wore a turban-styled head-covering to hide the stitches which were usually behind the ears, and then dark glasses to mask their bruised eyes, this only added to the mystery of their identities. Needless to say, Lady Mac also had her fair share of facial tweaks, and just as with her many convalescing guests would go through the same process, after which they all came out looking a million dollars - though as Lady M would always say whilst holding out her hands after one of her tweaks, 'These are the only things you can't fix, and they will always give you away in the end.'

    53 Glebe Place, as can be seen, was always a place to meet many varied and interesting people, but foremost amongst these must be her invaluable housekeeper, cook, confidante and friend, Lillian Todd, or Lill as we knew her. Lill is a small, tough but extremely gentle old-world London girl with the most genuinely happy and chirpy nature of anyone I have ever met, even though she has had more than her share of personal challenges, including being asthmatic, and even defeating cancer. Her happy nature has never faltered and is without a doubt the main reason for her longevity; the well-known saying: 'Always look on the bright side of life.' certainly works for her. She, in more ways than one, bears a resemblance to the cockney actress Irene Handel, for just like her, behind the simple façade there lays a very smart and sophisticated lady. For over thirty years Lill cared for Lady Mac, cooking for her and her guests many varied and sumptuous meals, while at the same time keeping house. This entailed not only general cleaning but also involved repairs of various household items, the sewing of clothing, and the polishing of

the vast amount of silver required for large dinner parties - this, Cyril and I would retrieve from the bank for these special occasions. Her work was always immaculate, for she was most sensitive to the many demands of her employer, who at times, as we knew only too well, could be quite a stickler for detail. Just like Cyril, with whom for obvious reasons she was a great friend, Lill still to this day remains most discreet about the many goings-on during her years with Lady Mac, and even though her friend and employer has now been dead for a number of years she will still not be drawn to reveal any of the many interesting things that she was witness to during this time ... now, that really is loyalty.

  Lady Mac was also a great provider of work for Cyril, for just like his other great benefactor, the wonderful Mrs G, she was also a talented interior decorator, and between them they would provide Cyril with the great majority of his business. These two Ladies, one by name and one by nature, would vie for Cyril's attention, and indeed, there was more than a little jealousy between them. This, at times, would take very sensitive handling, but Cyril would always manage to smooth over any bumps and make them both feel that they were top of his list. They were both extremely good at their work, and over the years we were to witness their unique and very individual styles many times. Mrs G was the master of the traditional English home, using beautiful fabrics and papers, all very solid but refined, whereas Lady Mac did her 'English' with a little more international flavour and pizazz, which really summed up the difference between them.

  But let's get back to the drug-crazed sixties. One day, Lady Mac took Cyril into her confidence, and asked for his assistance in acquiring the necessary illegal substances. Between them a plan was hatched to scour the pubs in Soho, as they, for some reason, believed this to be the most likely part of London for their plan to succeed. Cyril, as ever, rose to the challenge, and one evening they set off together - Lady Mac making a most convincing Lady Penelope, 'Step on it Parker', and Cyril, in his role of Parker the chauffeur, 'Yes, milady'. After what must have been, to put it mildly, quite an interesting journey which this most unlikely of couples went on in their quest through the pubs of Soho, they returned to Chelsea unscathed but successful, and now in possession of the required drugs - and as they say, 'Thunderbirds are Go!'

The party was to include a large number of Lady Mac's friends and would also include some of the most influential people in British society, none more so than the ex-Attorney General, Sir Hartley Shawcross, one of the most successful legal counsels of his day. Needless to say many of those present were clients of Cyril's, and Cyril was of course invited. As a boy I had met Sir Hartley upon several occasions when visiting him along with Cyril at his apartment in Knightsbridge, and had always found him just a little scary. He was a giant of a man and towered over Cyril, who was no shorty at 6ft 1 in., and his heavy Scottish brogue also made him sound rather stern; but it was his incredibly powerful presence that I found most disturbing, and it was no wonder, for he was the man that had looked into the eyes of some of the greatest evil that the world has ever seen: for he had had the unenviable task of being Chief Prosecutor of all the surviving Nazis at the Nuremberg trials. Strangely, he had also prosecuted the infamous George Haigh, the acid-bath murderer, whose path was also to cross Cyril's - but as far as I know neither of them were aware of this odd coincidence. On the night of the party, Cyril, thoroughly spruced up, left the Worlds End and set off to drive towards the posh end of the Kings Road. He turned into Glebe Place, where down at the far end the party was by now in full swing. As he headed down the road he became aware of someone racing towards him. Drawing closer he began to realise that there, in the full glare of his headlights and approaching fast, was a naked woman, and then, to his astonishment, he realised that he knew her, and recognised her as Lady Shawcross, the young wife of the ex-Attorney General.

This strange situation was just like a joke told on the radio by a favourite comedian of Cyril's, Max Miller, who was also known as the Cheeky Chappie. Max was the master of rude, and dressed in the most outrageous brightly-coloured costumes. His joke, which was to get him banned from the BBC, went something like this: 'I was walking through the countryside the other day, the sun was out and it was lovely and warm. I came across a narrow bridge over a river and started my way across. All of a sudden from the other side appeared a lady with not a stitch on, naked as the day she was born she was. Well, as I said, it was only a narrow bridge and as she charged toward me I was in a bit of a quandary - I didn't know whether to block her passage or toss myself off.'

Now Cyril, unlike Max, was in no quandary; he had the most wonderful instincts in a crisis, and immediately flew into action. He stopped the car, somehow managed to cover her with his raincoat, and then drove her back to god only knows what, for as far as he knew the whole house could be stark naked. With the lady in tow Cyril nervously rang the bell. The lady, who strangely had not been missed, was smuggled inside, and Cyril, who was always the height of discretion, left, so as to save any further embarrassment to the lady, or indeed her husband, but also, I believe, to avoid what to him must have appeared to be a full-scale orgy in full swing, and this he wished to have no part of. As they say, timing is everything, and it was never more so than with the very fortuitous arrival of Cyril at exactly the right moment in this quiet Chelsea street. The mind boggles at the kind of headlines which would have followed had things turned out otherwise.

Now Cyril, with his very strong morals, had kept this story to himself for many years, and only chose to share it with me whilst driving one morning through Chelsea after having just heard of the premature death of the young Lady Shawcross, who had been tragically killed whilst riding on the Sussex Downs. He explained that it would not have been right to talk about her whilst she was alive, but having now passed on he felt she was beyond harm. Cyril was most chivalrous in this way and a real ladies man.

Many years later, whilst walking along the same stretch of the Kings Road, I was amused to see what had now become quite a common sight - a naked male streaker, with a London bobby, helmet and all, in hot pursuit. Incredibly, they ran down Glebe Place, the very same street, creating a strange parody of Cyril's incident many years prior. Who knows, maybe a residue of that strange night had been left in this part of Chelsea, - but to my knowledge Lady Shawcross was most definitely the first streaker.

In January 1973, having just turned seventeen, I was about to take my long awaited driving test, for although I had been driving for some years this would allow me at last to do it legally. With my test just a few days away Cyril set me an interesting and most generous challenge: If I passed the dreaded test first time he would give me his car. With such a prize in sight how could I fail ... so I passed the test with flying colours, and found myself the proud owner of his green, three year old Vauxhall Victor 2000 Estate; but now Cyril would need a car himself, and this would come about in a most interesting way.

At the time Lady Mac, who was constantly fishing for financiers, or husbands, as she called them, had hooked a big fish from across the pond: a rich American who, for reasons that shall become clear will remain nameless; however, the prospective husband came with a twist. She confided to Cyril that this likeable chap had a problem with his private part, which was so bent he could not get it up, so Lady Mac, with her connections to plastic surgery, arranged for the required alterations. The American naturally got on well with Cyril, and so one afternoon over drinks at Glebe Place the story of Cyril's car was told, and after listening the American turned to Lady Mac and said, 'Connie, give the Jag to Mr D, and I'll buy you a new car.' So Cyril was now the owner of Lady Mac's Jaguar 420, or love and two kisses as she called it after the number plate, LXX 444; but Lady Mac, being canny as ever, far from giving the car to Cyril sold it to him. The surgery went ahead and was a complete success ... well, it was for the American who, now being firmly back in his stride, was to slip the hook, bolt from Lady Mac and desert her stable to return across the pond and into the arms of a much younger bride.

Cyril of course loved the Jag but he was also rather fond of being driven by me, and this would make the small matter of insurance extremely difficult, for being only seventeen at the time it proved to be almost impossible. Cyril though was not one to be thwarted, and eventually paid out £400, a small fortune in 1973, for my much delighted inclusion on his policy. So now I found myself with not only my own car but also the use of a 4.2 litre Jag. Not bad for a seventeen year old; I felt like Jack the lad.

There was to be one more occasion where pot was to play a part in the goings-on at Lady Macs, though in this instance she was to be blissfully unaware of its presence. In the summer of 1975 on a glorious but very hot day, I, along with my usual work partners, Alf and Eddie, were painting the outside of her lovely home. Being on the street meant that we were visible to most of the other residents of Glebe Place, and some of them would inevitably stop for a chat when passing. One afternoon two guys from the house next door appeared, and offered us each a can of beer. We never usually drank alcohol during working hours, but being as it was late afternoon and such a hot day we gratefully accepted their kind offer, and they joined us for a drink outside the house. The guys in question were both connected to Marc Bolan of T Rex fame, one being his manager and the other was the comically named Micky Finn, Bolan's partner in the band, who, whilst chatting with us, pulled out the inevitable joint. As was usual with pot the joint was shared, and so passed around, and to my surprise both Alf and Eddie, who had never tried it before, chose to give it a go … and then, right on cue, Cyril arrived in his Jag.

    Out he swaggered to immediately comment, 'Cor, this is alright, now I'm paying you to go on the booze.' and then added, 'Where's mine then?' Having received a beer of his own we returned to our social interlude and the joint was once again passed between the two musos. Now, Cyril never missed a trick, but having missed out on the aforementioned party he was a little naïve regarding the finer points of pot etiquette, and so naturally assumed that the two guys were sharing a cigarette. Being a generous soul he immediately thrust his hand into his pocket to pull out his pack of Silk Cut to 'splash the ash' or offer them around, stating, 'Is that all you've got? Here, have one of mine'. We all fell about laughing, partly from the effects of the pot but more from the wonderful innocence of Cyril's comment who, upon being put in the picture, needless to say joined in.

    Shortly after this Cyril was to quit smoking; this was no small thing for he had been a sixty-a-day man for most of his life which, as a consequence, had given him a cough to end all coughs. So one day whilst driving him, coughing as usual, along the Kings Road, he rolled down his window, scrunched up his pack of Silk Cut and launched them out of the window where they came to rest right outside Chelsea Town Hall. 'That's it I've quit!' he said. 'Oh yeah', I thought. But, surprisingly, that really was it, and he never smoked again.

Whilst on the subject of Cyril and cars, it's worth relating a couple of stories, one where Cyril by his quick thinking, was able to avoid what could have turned into an embarrassing and potentially disastrous situation. One afternoon, having been to a boozy lunch at the Kensington home of one of his clients, and being Cyril, having had quite a few in the process, he was stopped by a policeman on a motor bike. In the car with him was his good friend Lill, who he had agreed to drive home and who would now turn out to be the form of his salvation. As the policeman was dismounting from his bike Cyril told Lill to act as if she were in great pain, and upon being approached by the policeman Cyril's plan would now unfold. He wound down his window and went straight on the offensive. Shouting at the unfortunate officer he said, 'What do you think you're doing stopping me? Can't you see I've got a sick woman here and I'm trying to get her to the hospital!' Next to him sat Lill, writhing in agony for all she was worth, and her performance carried the day, for the policeman looked straight back at Cyril and said, 'I'm sorry sir', strapped on his helmet and said, 'Follow me.' With their police escort's lights flashing, Cyril and Lill were raced across Kensington and right into the grounds of St Mary Abbott's Hospital where, to their great relief, he turned to wave to them and went speeding off and on his way. What would have happened had he accompanied them inside we will never know...

One warm, sunny afternoon in the late 'sixties, Cyril was sat waiting at traffic lights in his car with his good friend and artist, Laurie Wrey. Laurie was a member of The Chelsea Arts Club and organiser of the Arts Club Ball, which was held annually at the Albert Hall. Being an artist he was also quite bohemian in style, and had a long flowing head of thick blond hair, which would be responsible for creating an interesting incident of mistaken identity upon that warm and sunny afternoon.

At the same time my mother, Joyce, just happened to be walking along the same stretch of the Kings Road, having just been shopping or 'up the shops' as she put it. Although she was a kind and intelligent woman she was also in possession of a fiery temper, which once roused would have most people running for cover -

something that Cyril from experience had quite sensibly learned to do very well. On spotting his car she saw sitting in HER front passenger seat what she took to be a blond bird and with HER husband; temper now roused, she swung her handbag and let it fly. It shot straight through the open window coming to rest against the blond head of the innocent and unwitting Laurie Wrey. Now, the contents of a ladies handbag have always been a bit of a mystery to those of the opposite sex, but these were now revealed, for there sat the unfortunate Laurie with lipsticks, lighters, cigarettes, compacts and the many other essential, and in some cases, unidentifiable items, previously contained within, now spilled all around, and in fact all over him. He exclaimed in a dazed shock, 'What the hell was that!' to which Cyril just replied, 'That was my wife'. Fortuitously the traffic lights had now changed, and Cyril, foot to the floor wasted no time in avoiding any further missiles from coming their way, and sped off to make his escape.

   Escaping may have seemed the wise thing to do at the time, but no matter how hard he tried to convince Joyce that he was with a man and not 'a blond bird', as she would have it, he would never succeed, and she remained adamant that he had been caught out with a girlfriend - and he was condemned once again to the dog-house. Needless to say, Laurie Wrey never accepted another lift from his good friend Cyril.

Cyril's father William aged around fifteen, working as a farrier in Glebe Place.

Cyril's mother Ellen.

Cyril's father William.

Cyril with his Father William around 1925.

Cyril with his Mother Ellen around 1926.

Cyril with his Father William around 1929.

Pub outing in a charabanc

Young Cyril out with the boys looking like bootleggers.

VE day celebration in Slaidburn St. My Aunt Emma is at the front and an effigy of Hitler is hanging from the Weatherby Arms behind her.

Coronation party in Slaidburn St.1952

The winner of the minstrel contest

Coronation slap up. Cyrils mother Ellen is on the far right holding the tray.

Cyril at the centre (in the light suit) with his workmen. His brother Pat is to his left and Bill Marriot the reformed monarchist is standing behind them.

Yet another Pub outing.

Mum with Sue and Carol watched by urchins outside a shabby 17 Slaidburn St.

Pauline, Sue and Carol and not to forget Muffin the mule.

Happy days. Joyce with Cyril and his brother Fred.

Battersea Fun Fair. Carol, Pete and Sue with friends, Eileen and Jeannie Smith.

Cyril with Carol, Sue and Pete at a holiday camp.

Billy Lowe, Aunt Dolly, Nanny Barnes and Tommy the dog.

The three Nannies, Nichols, Devenport and Barnes enjoying a beer.

Pete with Cyril and his first car an Austin van.

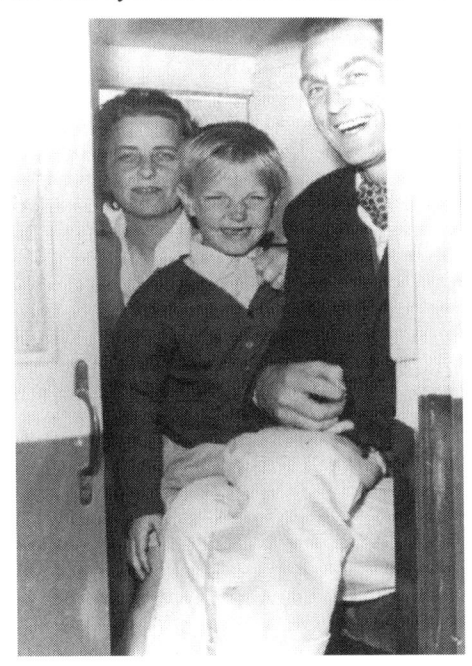

Pete with Joyce and Cyril on the Dymchurch railway.

Pete with Chairman Cyril outside the Chelsea Conservative Club.

The Staff of Carols Cafe. Karen, Maisie, Cyril, Carol and Sue.

Cyril in drag, raising funds for a worthy cause.

Cyril as drawn so accurately by a customer at the cafe.

CHAPTER NINE

GET OUT OF THAT

*A first-rate organizer is never in a hurry. He is never late.
He always keeps up his sleeve a margin for the unexpected.*
-Arnold Bennett.

Cyril had the most incredible ability to salvage what to most of us would be irretrievable situations, and these particular stories involve a couple of his great escapes.

One morning, in the late 1960s, a team of our workmen arrived at Slaidburn Street to load the equipment and materials required for Cyril's latest job, which was in South Audley Street, Mayfair. At this time we had a gated yard just up the street, which was the site of a bombed house that had been destroyed during the blitz. In the yard we kept all of our large equipment: ladders, wooden planks, scaffolding etc. We also had a paint and wallpaper store which was on the ground floor of another house in the street which used to be a little shop run by a Mrs Christmas, and was, conveniently, almost opposite our home. The paint store was filled mostly with stock of different kinds, and was where we kept the spare paints and wallpapers for the many houses that we had worked upon; these were all labelled, in the event that they may be needed to make repairs in the future. In those days all coloured paint had to be hand mixed, as the mixing machines that we are now so familiar with did not exist, and so Cyril, being a master at making and matching colour, would create the many different shades of paints, which would all be unique, to the many clients for whom he worked over the years. The van was loaded and the men were given their instructions as usual over a cup of tea in our kitchen, the job being to redecorate the entrance hall and staircase of the five-storey Mayfair house. Having finally given them the address Cyril sent them on their way, and said he would see them there, or so he thought, in a couple of hours.

The clients were American, and, as was common with many of our jobs, they were sensibly having the work carried out whilst visiting their family in the U.S.A. Two hours later, just as planned, Cyril and I arrived at the house in South Audley Street outside which, as expected, stood our sign-written van. We rang the bell, and the door was opened by the maid.

The maid was a glorious sight: she was a lovely, big, round, black mumma, wearing a white dress with white pumps and socks, which contrasted wonderfully with her very smooth and dark skin; she looked like she had just walked off the set of *Gone With The Wind*. With a huge smile upon her colourful face she said, in her lovely soft way-down-South American accent, 'Well, good morning Mr Devenport. Come on in.' - and welcomed us into a very empty house.

Cyril remarked, 'Where are my men?'

'I don't know Mr. Devenport, they have sure not been here.' she replied.

Cyril was perplexed, for the van stood outside and after peering through its windows was found to be completely empty; it had been unloaded - but unloaded to where? Cyril being Cyril, sprang straight into action and took to the middle of the road and began shouting out the names of his missing workmen, 'Alfie, Eric, Tommy!' into this exclusive and once peaceful neighbourhood. After a while the door of the adjoining house opened, and there stood Eric, one of the painters, in his white bib and braces with a confused look upon his face. Cyril with his hands on his hips said, 'What are you doing in there?'

Eric replied, 'Stripping the staircase'.

The colour drained from Cyril's face, and we entered the house to be confronted by his team of men who had wasted no time in removing a large part of the wallpaper from the staircase as instructed, but from the wrong house. After much agitated talk it was discovered that not only had Cyril given them the wrong house number, but the owners, who by coincidence also happened to be Americans, were themselves back in the U.S.A. Incredibly, their maid, God only knows why, had welcomed the workmen in and left them to begin the destruction of her employer's home. Cyril was in quite a fix, and taking the only course open to him he telephoned our clients in America, who fortunately for us happened to be good friends with their neighbours. Armed now with their telephone number he set about the unenviable task of informing them of his mistake. After much apologising from Cyril they informed him, much to his relief, that everything was 'just fine', and went on to say that the hall and staircase were a bit shabby and in desperate need of decoration; so, incredibly, they requested that he stay on and finish the job. Cyril was flabbergasted.

And so it turned out that we redecorated the entrance hall and the staircase of two houses in South Audley Street (buy one get one free). Yet again Cyril had found a way out of a most embarrassing and potentially costly situation, and, as was usual, had even managed against all the odds to turn it to his advantage.

But the fun was not over yet. Whilst working in the wrong house, our workmen, on their way to repair a flat roof which was two stories up at the back of the building, had unknowingly carried a leaking pot of tar up the long staircase. The staircase was fitted with a bright red Wilton carpet which we had of course covered with dust sheets, but these were no match for the tar. The leaking pot had dripped intermittently all the way up the stairs, and the tar had managed to soak through the protecting sheets and find its way through to the expensive bright red Wilton underneath, leaving dark, ugly stains every third or fourth tread all the way up to the second-floor. Once again, Cyril, though exasperated, sprang straight into action. A man was sent for a five gallon drum of turpentine and Cyril had the carpet lifted; it was then raised up over boards placed between step ladders to form tents, so the turpentine could be poured through into a bucket underneath. Cyril was insistent that the tar must not be touched, and continued to pour the turpentine until all of the tar was washed through. The carpet was then sent to be cleaned – and, when returned and refitted, it looked immaculate. The final twist was when Cyril informed the client that he had taken the liberty of having the carpet cleaned as it looked a bit tired against the newly decorated staircase. The client was delighted and praised Cyril for his initiative, and happily paid for its cleaning. . . . Cyril had done it again.

One last calamity awaited us in South Audley Street whilst fitting a new kitchen in the basement of the right house. Now, Americans were used to their kitchens being fitted with appliances large enough to live in, and these could only be imported from the good old U.S.A., ours being deemed totally inadequate for their needs. Compared to our tiny and very basic domestic versions theirs were like ocean liners with all the trimmings, and each one, being American, would require its own transformer to convert it to our higher electric current. In went a massive cooker, a vast washing-machine, a tumble-drier and a cavernous Westinghouse fridge-freezer, complete with a built in ice-maker, which required it to be plumbed, like the washing machine, into the water supply.

At this time in the U.K. kitchens were pretty basic; not everyone had a fridge, freezers were almost unheard of, and even fewer people had washing machines, which were considered the height of luxury; so you can imagine our amazement as these vast machines were put in place - we were just like kids in a toyshop. Everything was fitted and all was well, or so we thought, and off we went for the night.

The next morning we arrived to find the kitchen flooded, and protruding from the now open door of the huge fridge-freezer was an avalanche of ice. It turned out that a small arm in the ice collector, which was designed to stop the production of the ice, had not been fitted, so the machine, in its efficient and energetic American way, had continued pumping out ice all night long to form what must surely have been the first ever glacier in Mayfair. After shovelling up the ice and mopping up the copious amount of water all was well. Luckily, no damage had been done, and with the missing arm now in place the huge Westinghouse fridge-freezer now worked beautifully.

Cyril was very pleased to see the back of South Audley Street, and, as usual, was able to see the funny side of the whole experience, which he had so cleverly turned from potential loss into glorious profit.

Some years later Cyril's amazing knack of getting out of the most difficult situations would be further tested once again, and, as ever, he seemed almost instinctively to know exactly what to do when faced with any kind of potential catastrophe.

In 1982, I was working once again with two of our workmen, Alf and Eddie, at the Bank of New York in Leadenhall Street, opposite the wonderful old Leadenhall Market in the City of London. The bank, being a Merchant bank, dealt mostly with large national and international business transactions, so it was quite unlike the banks which we are familiar with on our high streets.

You entered into a huge banking-hall in which there were around twenty desks, behind each of which sat various advisers along with their secretaries; it was here that most of the bank's business was carried out. It was beautifully decorated with silk panels and antique furnishings, which were all carefully chosen and supplied by another of Cyril's talented lady decorators, the charming Barbara Brocklebank.

Mrs B was a very sensitive and talented decorator, who had a particular liking for all things turquoise, and over the many years that we worked with her I believe that we must have explored every possible shade and variation of this vibrant colour. She was most exacting in her work, which had always to be carried out with great precision. This was clearly evident with her own appearance which, as you would expect, was very smart right down to the smallest detail, which included the tiniest, most perfectly painted flowers which she applied daily to her eyelids as part of her make-up.

We were responsible for all decoration and maintenance in the bank, all to be carried out to Mrs B's exacting requirements. Upon this occasion we were redecorating the director's dining-room, in which was a large oak dining-table: this had also been supplied by Mrs B, and being eighteenth century was rather valuable.

Having covered the room thoroughly with sheeting we set about our work. Somehow, that morning, a cup of tea was spilt on the table, which although covered, quickly soaked through the sheets, and being hot, left a large white patch on the surface of this very valuable piece of furniture. As we stood pondering what to do next the sound of Cyril's signature whistle could be heard approaching the room, for providentially he had arrived for his daily job inspection right on cue. Upon seeing the damaged table he sprang straight into action.

I was despatched to buy eighty cigarettes, a pint of linseed oil and a bottle of vinegar. When I returned Cyril tore open a pack of the cigarettes and instructed us all to light up and to keep smoking them one after another, his aim being to collect the ash, which we all dutifully flicked into a small pot. In no time at all the dining-room was filled with clouds of smoke, and resembled more a night-club than a dining-room. We consumed fag after fag, the whole time being geed up by Cyril to keep on puffing, even imploring us to smoke two at a time. After a while (thankfully for us), he had acquired enough cigarette ash for his plan, which to us still remained a complete mystery.

He instructed me to boil the kettle, while he was in the process of mixing the cigarette ash with vinegar and linseed oil into a strange grey paste. Once boiling he grabbed the kettle, and to our complete horror poured the boiling water all over the table top. The whole thing now turned pale, and I thought, 'You've really done it now Cyril.' Next, he poured his secret weapon, the strange grey paste onto the table top, and handing us rags instructed us to polish it in. This we did for about thirty minutes, puffing and blowing as we went, which was not only from the exertion but also the after effects of an intense and serious smoking session. To our amazement the table started to come back to life, its colour returning, and applying a bit more elbow grease we gave it a good buffing, and it came up as good as new.

Where he had learnt this trick I never did find out, but, as ever, he always seemed able to find the most original and effective solutions for the most difficult of situations

Whilst on all things American, some years prior to this, an American family moved into Slaidburn Street. They were affectionately known by us Worlds Enders as 'The Yanks', and, compared to us impoverished Londoners, they seemed as if they had come from another planet. The father was a Colonel in the U.S. Air Force, and because of this the family's provisions were delivered in bulk by a massive truck from the U.S. Air Base. There were steaks the size of half a cow, not just tins of beans but whole cases, proper burgers, which bore no resemblance to the piddly Wimpeys that we were more accustomed to, hot dogs, crates of coca cola and many bottles of Bourbon. These were just some of the things that were unloaded before our hungry eyes, and gave us all a sneak preview of the shape of things to come.

Just to prove that they really were from outer space, outside their house stood the biggest car that had ever been seen in Slaidburn Street - a metallic pale blue Cadillac with huge wings at the back, just like a rocket. They had a son called Terry, who was around my age; he was an archetypal U.S. Air Force child of the time, with buck-teeth, cropped G.I. haircut and the loudest voice (biggest mouth) in the street, and for a short time we were friends.

One thing I remember about their time with us involved the kids in the street cramming into the cavernous boot of the spaceship-like Cadillac in order to see how many of us could fit in. I think about ten of us managed to squeeze ourselves in, all screaming and laughing, and it was still possible to close the lid.

The Americans stayed in the street for about a year, and were quite a novelty. . . . One can only wonder what they made of us.

There is one last thing to add to my story of all things American. Whilst typing this story in my home, which is in the hills of North Wales, I became aware of the approaching sound of what I assumed to be a Spitfire. This rare and beautiful machine is owned by a local enthusiast, and he often takes it for a spin over the high moors. This is such a wonderful sight, and, as was usual, I rushed outside leaving my pc, to try to catch a glimpse of this glorious bird. I was just in time to see, not the expected Spitfire, but another veteran aircraft of World War Two - a fully restored Harvard T6 with its U.S. Air Force markings clearly visible on the underside, just a few hundred feet above my home... a very strange coincidence indeed.

CHAPTER TEN

HOSPITAL JOB

*Whereas it has long been known and declared
that the poor have no right to the property of the rich,
I wish it also to be known and declared
that the rich have no right to the property of the poor.*
-John Ruskin.

The early 1970s were a tumultuous time in Britain: the economy was in recession and there were more strikes than found in a large box of matches. The most visible of these just had to be the dustmen, which left London with ever increasing piles of stinking rubbish building up all over the place. Power cuts also added to the disturbance that our dear old country went through at this time, and these made working life particularly difficult, especially during the short hours of daylight during a British winter, but on the upside they did help to conceal all the rubbish.

All of these factors made the task of running a business even more difficult, but fortunately for us Cyril had secured work that would take us through the winter months ahead, which were always the most trying time in the building industry. The substantial job in hand would require us to completely refurbish a large eight-bedroom house in Kensington, and was referred to by Cyril as a 'Hospital Job'. The meaning of this term referred not only to the size and duration of the job, but its ability to get us through difficult times - especially during winter, keeping all of the men employed whilst allowing us a certain freedom to go back and forth to work on any other smaller jobs that would need to be done along the way; this was very important if you wished to keep all of your clients happy.

The beginning of the saga of this large town-house was to involve a typical piece of Cyril's ingenuity and cunning. We, as usual, inspected the run-down house with the clients, in order for Cyril to give it his professional eye and supply the prospective owners with a general idea of the amount of work which would be required. Now, Cyril was not a qualified surveyor, but in fact was much more than that, for being the builder he would be the man upon whom all responsibility for the work ahead would fall; his knowledge was so great that he acted in his roll of surveyor for many of our clients. The less trusting of them would, to their regret and expense, employ a qualified surveyor, only to be told exactly, or sometimes less than, what he had told them for free. In his role of surveyor he would roam around, thumping upon walls, stamping upon floors and poking at woodwork with a small pocket knife which he always carried. Up would come floorboards, and he would cast his beady eye upon almost everything inside and out, before giving his expert opinion of the general condition and the amount of work to be expected. It was great to watch this large man, who always wore a suit and tie, go about his work: he was never afraid of getting his hands dirty, and would tear down wallpaper, lift drains and climb right onto roof tops with great ease, all the time making light of it, and giving us a few laughs along the way.

  Having given the house the 'thumbs up', the next stage of the process could begin. This required many visits with all of the different tradesmen: plumbers, electricians etc., in order that an estimate of costs and a schedule of work could be prepared. My favourite part of all of this was always the laying out of the bathrooms. Of course, this required the clients to be present; Cyril was in his element and would place himself in all sorts of contorted positions around the empty rooms, demonstrating how the imaginary baths, bidets and toilets would fit into its different parts. The bidets or 'biddys', as he called them, always raised a good laugh, as he would squat down, thankfully keeping his trousers up, and then pretend to use them. Estimates were completed, submitted and accepted, and the date was set for the start of the job.

  About two weeks before we were due to start work we received a call from the client, who was much distressed, and informed us that the house had been taken over by squatters. This was a very common occurrence in the 1970s, and was usually carried out by students taking advantage of the large amount of empty property that was part of London at this time. This created quite a problem for us, and, although we had sympathy for the young squatters, we could not afford to have them interrupt the tight schedules involved in the upcoming work, which could even put in jeopardy the whole future of the much valued 'Hospital Job'. Cyril assured the client that he would deal with the problem, and we set off immediately for Kensington.

Now, I had no idea what he intended to do, but knew that somehow he would sort out this awkward mess, which conceivably could go on for months if dragged into the courts, requiring eviction orders as part of the legal process - all taking precious time that neither he nor the client could afford.

Upon arrival he marched up the steps of the house and proceeded to bang the shining brass lion-headed knocker on the large black front door. After some time it was eventually opened, and we were confronted by a young man who looked like, and probably had, just crawled out of bed. He looked at us and announced, 'You can't come in here, we've got squatter's rights.

Quick as a flash, Cyril replied, 'That may well be my boy, but I'm the builder and I'm due to start work here this week'.

Cyril then looked over the young man's shoulder and exclaimed, 'What's happened to all my stuff! I left twenty gallons of paint here. And where are my steps and equipment?' Now, all this was pure invention, something that he did quite spontaneously, and it left me almost as confused as the squatter. The squatter reeled back in alarm, and claimed total ignorance of any materials.

At this point Cyril said, 'You'd better let me in to have a look round'.

In we went, Cyril stomped around, pretending to look for his imaginary paint and equipment, stating as he went that he'd left such and such here and such and such there – which, of course, were now not there. He then told the squatter that he would have to get the police, as there had been a theft committed. At this point the squatter began to panic and denied all knowledge of any materials being there. Cyril knew then that he had him. He told him that he believed his story and was sure that he had played no part in the theft, but would only not contact the police if all of the squatters agreed to leave the house. This was settled, and Cyril, being the generous guy that he was, even allowed them a few days grace to find someone else's house to squat in.

The client was as amazed as I was at Cyril's inventiveness, and was most grateful to him for relieving them of what could have been a most difficult and costly problem.

After many months the house was now restored to its splendid original condition, all beautifully decorated to a very high standard throughout, and, having built and fitted a beautiful hand-made kitchen, there was just one thing left to complete the work. This involved the laying of an imported floor in the kitchen which was to be carried out, not by us, but by the suppliers themselves. We had spent the final (or so we thought) morning clearing all of our equipment from the house, and having literally taken the last stepladder out to the waiting van outside, Cyril and I were stood at the front door saying our goodbyes to the grateful clients. It was a lovely sunny morning, and we were all in high spirits ... but not for long.

All of a sudden, there was the most almighty bang from within the house. We all looked back across the large entrance-hall with its beautiful sweeping staircase and baby grand piano, to the far end toward the kitchen door. We now realised that it had been the slamming shut of the door which had been partly responsible for the huge bang. The door slowly opened, to reveal the tall, moustached figure of the workman who had been laying the floor, who slowly staggered out into the hall looking very dazed. Billowing all around him and pouring out of the kitchen came a fog of the finest black soot that I have ever seen; the air was literally filled with it. We rushed across the hall to him and saw that his hair, moustache and eyebrows were all singed and he had lost all the hair on his arms, which were lightly but not badly burnt. Luckily, apart from being a little shocked he was generally all right. Meanwhile, this fine soot was floating all around us, and, much to our horror, all around this newly completed house.

It transpired that he had been using a new, very strong adhesive and the fumes from it built up to a point where they had been ignited by the pilot flame of the brand new hob, which he had failed to check and extinguish prior to using this extremely inflammable glue. Gas appliances at this time all had these perpetually burning flames, even the expensive top-of-the-market ones. We walked together throughout the house and found that the soot had literally gone everywhere, getting onto and sticking to all the curtains and carpets, onto the fabric of the numerous antique sofas and chairs, into built-in wardrobes, covering the shoulders of all the clothes hanging within, and even reaching up to the third floor where a washing-machine had been running in the nursery. When the clothes came out they were all grey.

Our next step was to unload our equipment straight back into the house in order to begin the process of cleaning up the unbelievable mess that had been created by this small, but very costly, oversight. All carpets and curtains had to be cleaned, and all of the clothing in the house was also sent off for cleaning. Silk wallpaper had to be replaced in certain rooms, and almost all the house had to be washed clean in one way or another. The beautiful hand-built kitchen, which had been finished with a specialist paint effect, had been scorched in places and required complete redecoration. We were to spend a further six weeks putting all of the damage right; it was a very expensive mistake which, fortunately, was not ours, and which resulted in a large insurance claim to cover the substantial cost of returning the house to normal.

A small matter of interest regarding this house, and the ever-changing value of property in this particular part of London - our clients purchased the house in early 1974 for the sum of £80,000. The major work required to restore the house cost them a further £65,000. In 1977 they sold the house with great difficulty, due to the deepening economic woes being experienced in the U.K. at the time, for the sum of £125,000, giving them a net loss of around £20,000. In 2003 the same house was on the market for £3,000,000 - yes, I do mean million. Finally, at the time of writing, I found an almost identical house in the same road for the bargain price of, wait for it - £8.5 million. As they say: 'If I only knew then what I know now'.

CHAPTER ELEVEN

BLEAK HOUSE

Regrets are the natural property of grey hairs.
-Charles Dickens

The winter of 1973 was spent refurbishing a once grand, but now very dilapidated, six-bedroom house in west London. It was in a quiet cul-de-sac off Barnes Common, and was less than one hundred yards from the spot where Mark Bolan was so unfortunately killed in 1977.

The first work we did on the house was the plumbing and the stripping out of all the wiring. On top of this, all of the floors on the ground level were also removed due to dry rot; so for a few months the house was to be rather uncomfortable. It was a particularly cold winter that year, and having no form of heating and only bare ground to walk on downstairs, it created a lot of complaints from the many workmen there, and resulted in their naming it 'Bleak House'.

The house had been bought by a well-known impresario as part of the divorce settlement from his young wife Sarah. Sarah was the mother of his two children, and, having retired from her very successful career as a top fashion model, was at this time somewhere around her mid-thirties. She was a very beautiful girl, with auburn hair and stunning green eyes, and had appeared in many TV commercials, and was also often seen around London on large advertising billboards.

After some very uncomfortable months Bleak House had been transformed, with all the major work, such as heating, floors etc., completed, much to the relief of our workmen, and many of the rooms had now been decorated. This made it possible for Sarah to move in, her plan being to oversee the final decoration of the house. It soon became clear to all of us working there that all was not well with Sarah, for she had a most serious drink problem ... and her alcoholism was to create a most unusual and unorthodox working relationship.

Things were O.K. for a short while, but soon her drinking began to get out of control, and as a result she began to struggle to keep things together in the house. Her solution was to employ as an assistant, one of our painters, a chap called Eric, who looked rather like Sid James, and at times could be just as witty. His day would start by making breakfast for the children, driving them to school and then returning to spend the rest of the day to sit talking and drinking with Sarah; this created quite a stir with the rest of the workmen, and Eric had to put up with a lot of ribbing from all of us, for, as you might imagine, we were all more than a little envious of his unorthodox, but very cushy working day.

At this time Sarah was being treated by one of London's top psychoanalysts who, though employed to treat her, had during their sessions quite understandably fallen for her. We had all but finished our work upon the house when Sarah announced that her new beau, the psychoanalyst, was to move in.

He was a most striking character, being all of 6 ft 5 in., of Asian origin and every bit the dominant male. His first action was to inform us that he would like us to convert the attic of the house. Now, having just completed most of our work and redecoration and the house now being as bright as a new pin, this struck us as a strange request, but, being a dominant male, I suppose he was marking out his territory. Being such a tall man we were also required to custom-build an enormous bed for him, which when completed allowed him to move into the house proper.

He turned out to be a complete control freak (being a shrink I suppose he would be, wouldn't he?), and we were required to consult him on even the smallest of details. This led to a memorable event when, early one morning, I found myself knocking upon his bedroom door for instructions. The door slowly opened to reveal quite an apparition: there he stood, all 6 feet 5 inches. of him, wearing a full-length, white cotton Victorian nightdress with a white bed cap complete with a bobble, from under which his large dark moustachioed face stared down at me. And just to round it all off upon his huge feet he was wearing a pair of equally huge red Turkish slippers, all covered in sparkles, which turned up at the toes into a tight curl. The sight before my eyes left me just a little speechless and I could hardly contain myself – but somehow I did manage to accomplish my mission, without cracking up, but only just.

I couldn't wait to tell the other workmen what I had just seen, and, as you would imagine, it made for a good laugh when we were all together at the next tea-break. Of course, the effect of this was quite predictable upon the men, for now they all just had to see the apparition for themselves. This led to any, or all of them, knocking upon his door first thing in the morning with the most trivial of questions - something that was done more than once - and always gave us all a great laugh.

Over the next couple of months he was to have us redecorate certain parts of the house to be more, as he put it, in keeping with his valuable collection of paintings and etchings; but I feel there was an element of top-dogging going on as he continued to further mark out his territory. This collection of art would be rotated around the house in ever-changing positions, to await his final approval on the place in which they were to be hung; incidentally, they never were, but they sure moved around a lot. He also instructed us to build a garage to house his latest gift to Sarah, which was a brand new Citroen Safari Estate. The garage did not last very long. One day, Sarah, who by this time was being kept more or less a house-prisoner with a full time live-in nurse, had managed to sneak off with the car keys, and, in attempting to escape had reversed the brand new car straight through the brand new brick wall of the brand new garage. ... He that must be obeyed, was not amused.

Sarah's nurse, who was also to act as a kind of gaoler, denying her any access to the car and especially to alcohol, did her best to control her, but Sarah like all addicts could be most cunning, and so would on many occasions escape to satisfy her terrible addiction. All of this had had quite an effect on the big shrink; Sarah had driven him almost to despair, and his inability to reform her caused him to act ever more strangely.

One day we were summoned to his office in Hans Place, Knightsbridge, its window overlooking Harrods, in order to settle his final account, for as he was to tell us, he had washed his hands of Sarah, and any further work to the house would have to be paid for by her. Cyril and I along with our foreman, Eric (her paid companion) were sat opposite him. He was most imposing behind his large antique desk with the backdrop of Harrods through the window behind him. He knit-picked his way through our bill of works, and this required one or all of us explaining or justifying every expense. It was a slow and tedious process, but things were about to liven up for suddenly the door opened, and in walked his secretary carrying a large Harrods box, beautifully wrapped and finished with a ribbon.

'This has just arrived for you, Mr Khan.' she said, and placed it upon his desk.

He opened the accompanying card, his face reddened, and then contorted, and he threw the card aside; he tore off the wrapping, removed the lid from the box and threw that aside also. Seemingly unaware of our presence he walked around from behind his desk and placed the box on the floor, which we could now see contained a large birthday cake. Last of all, he removed his shoes, jumped into the box and proceeded to jump up and down whilst shouting 'Fuck the cake, fuck the cake!' over and over.

Cyril, along with myself and Eric were dumbstruck as we watched this giant of a man bouncing up and down in the large cake, the result of which was that the sponge, cream and icing made its way over his socks and up his legs, to smother his pinstriped suit trousers. He was in one hell of a mess. Having vented his anger, he then casually stepped out of the box and returned to his seat behind his desk as if nothing had happened, and said, 'I am sorry Mr. Devenport, but it is my birthday and that was from *her*.'

We concluded our business, and were duly presented with his cheque of final payment. Sarah had certainly rattled his cage.

We somehow managed to make it out of the building and onto the street where we all fell about with much needed laughter. Cyril remarked, 'Think how much people pay him to sort out their heads, and he's a complete fruitcake.' This made us laugh all the more.

Our journey with Sarah was not quite over yet for there was still work to finish at the house which, upon completion, would see her disappear, leaving us with an unpaid bill for £5000 – a considerable sum of money at this time.

Cyril and I put on our Holmes and Watson hats, and after a few weeks we somehow managed to track her down to a flat in St. Johns Wood. Sarah, as ever, was most charming, apologising to Cyril and requesting his help in selling the house. She informed us that her next-door neighbour in Barnes had made an unreasonable offer to her, and Cyril, being the ladies' man that he was, knew that the chap was trying to take advantage of the lady: he would never stand for that.

A meeting was arranged with the neighbour, in order for Cyril to put him right and to explain the considerable work that had been done to the house; so, one evening we set off for Barnes. We arrived at Sarah's around 7 p.m., and over more than a few drinks made plans before the 8 p.m. meeting next door.

Cyril departed, leaving me with Sarah to chat and be entertained, as she attempted to teach me Yoga, at which she was most adept. After about an hour Cyril returned, and explained how, over a few more whiskies, he had put the neighbour straight, and had then got him to agree to Sarah's asking price for the house. Sarah was delighted, and this of course, required a celebration, and, naturally, more drinking ensued. They sat together, side by side on the sofa like two old friends, arms around each other, with many kisses on the cheek. It was all very jolly.

It was now nearly 10 o'clock, and definitely time to get Cyril home while he could still walk. Having politely called an end to the proceedings, and after many more hugs, kisses, thankyous and goodbyes, Cyril began unsteadily to rise - and then dramatically to fall. He crashed down on to the low table which was in front of him, sending a large china lamp which was upon the table flying across the room, to break into many pieces. Cyril was now on his hands and knees, and I watched aghast as he crawled from the room, still cheery and saying his goodbyes. I had never seen him so drunk; I apologised to Sarah, and she just laughed it all off and told me to get him home safely - he had more than met his match.

We drove back to Chelsea, Cyril puffing and blowing at my side, and as we turned into our street he instructed me to park away from the house because, as he put it, 'You'd better not let your mother see me like this.' I parked the car further up the street and then he said, 'Come and help me out, and walk me up and down a bit.' This was easier said than done, for Cyril was a big man, but nevertheless, I proceeded to get him out of the car. Having got him upright I held on to him tightly and doing just as he suggested walked him back and forth a few times; we must have been quite a sight. Turning towards the house for about the fifth time he then said to me, 'You go ahead and open the door, I'll come in, say goodnight and go straight to bed.'

Well, that was the plan, but I knew quite well that as our street door opened straight into our sitting room he would most certainly have an audience for his arrival.

I entered the house first, and there, as expected, sat my mother, accompanied by two of my sisters, Pauline and Karen and my brother-in-law Raymond. My mother asked, 'Where's your father?'

'He's coming.' I said.

In he marched, and looking straight ahead trying his best to avoid eye contact announced, 'I'm a bit tired, I think I'll go straight to bed. Goodnight all.'

With all eyes upon him he set off up the staircase. It was a brave attempt but all in vain for he only made it about half way up, at which point his footing failed, and down he came again with a crash.

My mother looked across and calmly announced, 'He's drunk.' … and we all roared with laughter.

I helped him to his feet, led him up the stairs and put him safely into bed. 'Sweet dreams, Dad.'

As promised, we received our final cheque from Sarah. She was a lovely person, and I really hope that her life became a better one, and she learned to be as good to herself as she was to all of us.

CHAPTER TWELVE

THE EXORCIST

*There are more things in Heaven and Earth, Horatio,
than are dreamt of in your philosophy'*
-William Shakespeare. '

Over the years, working in so many houses all over London, we were to experience some very strange things: apparitions, voices, workmen feeling that they were being watched, or even at times being touched by invisible hands.

Upon such occasions the unfortunate workmen would often be seen fleeing from the house in terror. It seems that making alterations to some of these old properties acts as a kind of trigger for events that can only be described as paranormal, whether it is some form of energy trapped in the fabric of the building that for some unknown reason is released, or just the disapproval of tenants past to any kind of change. The answer to this we will probably never find out, for these unexplained events are never predictable; but one thing is for sure, none of us involved in the story that follows will ever forget Cadogan Place.

In 1984, we were called by one of our regular clients who I will refer to as Mrs N. Mr and Mrs N were, at this time, in their late fifties; they were an attractive couple, and it was always a pleasure to work for them. We had been their builder-decorators for over twenty years, and, just as were many of Cyril's clients, they were also good friends. Their flat was in one of the best parts of Chelsea, in Cadogan Place, just off Sloane Street. These grand five-storey buildings were once one large dwelling, complete with a smaller mews house at the back which was used for staff, cars or carriages; but just like many of the grand houses in this part of London, over the years they have been converted into apartments.

On arriving at the flat we were welcomed by the lovely Mrs N, who then proceeded to show us the brand new burglar-alarm system which had just been fitted. This included movement detectors in all the rooms, and steel gates to all the windows. Mrs N then made rather an odd request, asking us if we would check throughout the flat for any kind of secret entrances or trap doors. This involved Cyril and I sounding floors, and moving furniture from walls to see if there was any possible way, other than the usual, that the flat could be entered. I must say that we found this all a bit strange, but we went about doing just as we were asked - to find, as expected, absolutely nothing. As was the custom when visiting the Ns, we proceeded to the drawing room where Cyril and Mrs N would sit and chat over their customary glass of whisky.

Mrs N was definitely not her usual calm and composed self, and appeared to be quite nervous. She then, hesitatingly, for she was obviously feeling rather awkward, went on to tell us that the flat was being plagued by some very strange occurrences. At first, there were a number of attacks to various pieces of furniture, which they would find upon their returning home. These involved tables and chairs being gouged with tools: screwdrivers, chisels etc., taken from their own tool box which was kept in a hall closet. The tools were always found close by the damaged furniture.

The next occurrence, and by far the most disturbing incident, was when upon returning home early one afternoon, Mrs N, on entering her bedroom, found it in complete chaos. She was alarmed to find all of her clothes had been taken from drawers and closets, and were now sprawled around the room and across her bed, and upon them there was a white, milky substance.

At this point the police were called, and after questioning Mrs N they decided to pay a visit to a chap known to Cyril and myself who had worked for them over many years as a handy-man. He was taken to Chelsea Police Station, and wrongly accused of being the perpetrator of these strange events, it being assumed that somehow he had managed to make copies of the keys to the flat, with which he had gained entrance. He protested his innocence, vehemently denying all the accusations. He was so disturbed by the experience that this rather nice and simple soul ultimately suffered a nervous breakdown.

A few weeks passed, and we were once again summoned to the flat for a meeting with Mrs N. She informed us that all of the new security measures that had been put in place were to no avail as the damage to the furniture was continuing, and the whole thing was upsetting her so much that she felt it was time to leave. Having made her decision she had in fact already moved out and so we would be required to generally tidy up the décor in order for the flat to be put on the market. She then went on to ask us to visit the flat occasionally to water the plants etc., as she now had no wish to be there, even temporarily. We were given a set of keys and then Mrs N and Cyril sat down for what was to turn out to be, though neither of them knew it at the time, their final glass of whisky together.

The following week, Cyril and I set off with two of our decorators (Alf and Eddie), for Cadogan Place. We took them into the flat and showed them the various jobs that were to be done. Both of these men were known well to us, and had worked for Cyril for many years. Alf was in his fifties, a very likeable chap and an experienced decorator. He was always great to work with, for he would croon his way through the day singing a collection of great old songs with his good clear voice. In fact, many of our clients, especially the females, would request his presence when work was to be done for them, enjoying his easy-going manner, and always complementing him upon his singing. As will now transpire, he was not to do very much crooning that day.

Eddie was some years younger than Alf, an innocent and likeable chap himself, but of a rather more nervous disposition.

Having given them their instructions I then left with Cyril, to visit the client whose house in Notting Hill they had just completed decorating. He was a whisky-distiller, and was so delighted with their work that he gave us two bottles of his own brand whisky, wrapped in gift-paper, to present to them. After what had been an uneventful but productive morning we headed back to the Worlds End, and home for an early lunch. As soon as we arrived my mother told us that Alf had been on the phone and sounded rather disturbed. He had insisted that we go directly to Cadogan Place as they had a problem. So after a hurried lunch washed down with a cup of tea we set off once again for Cadogan Place.

Upon arriving we were to find Alf and Eddie standing in the street outside the house. They were most agitated, and Alf's first remark was that they could not work in the flat because it was haunted. Now, this came as quite a surprise to me, for having known Alf since I was a boy, he had always insisted that my experiences and beliefs in ghosts were, as he put it, 'All in your head.' He would go on to say that he had been in the Navy during the Second World War, and having seen many terrible things, he had never seen a ghost or anything like one. I was rather pleased at this change of his beliefs; I had a good laugh, and told him to calm down and show us what on earth had been going on.

We marched into the entrance hall, led by Cyril, and followed rather reluctantly by our two workmen up to the first-floor flat, taking with us the two bottles of whisky which were still wrapped; these we placed upon a small table in the hall outside the drawing room. Alf led us into the drawing room where his step ladder stood just as he had left it, alongside the large book case, above which he had been working. He said that whilst up the ladder the music-system, which was directly below him, suddenly came on: loud music blared out, giving him such a fright he almost fell off the ladder. He climbed down, switched it off and looked for a timer. ...Well, there was no timer, and it became clear that the only way it could have come on was if it had been physically turned on; but as he had been alone in the room ... turned on by whom?

Whilst puzzling over this he, and Eddie who had now joined him, realised that there were voices coming from down the hall. They headed towards the voices, thinking there was someone in the flat. They unlocked the door to the second bathroom which was still locked from the outside, as was required for the alarm to be set, and entered to find no people but upon a shelf a portable radio blasting out an interview on Radio Four. Again, the only way in which the radio could be turned on was for someone, or something, to depress the switch on top! By now they were feeling a little perturbed, and set off back to the drawing room. Upon entering they noticed that across the room between the two large balcony windows at the front, the large oak cabinet, which was used for drinks and glasses, was now standing with its door wide open. Alf asked Eddie whether he had opened it, to which Eddie said 'no'. Alf went across and closed it, turning the key in the lock which secured the door. Out of the corner of his eye he saw something moving in the dining-room which adjoined the drawing-room and was connected by two large open doors. As he turned, to his horror, he saw the large crystal chandelier, which hung on a long chain over the large oak dining table, swinging like a pendulum. This was the final straw and they were both now completely rattled. Alf immediately telephoned and spoke to my mother, who then passed the message on to us upon our return home. They had both then hurriedly left the flat to wait outside for us to arrive.

Having explored the flat thoroughly, I must say that there was definitely a strange atmosphere hanging over the place, especially in the dining-room, where the air was noticeably chilled; but even more so at the far end of the corridor which came to a dead end as it met the next door property: here, there seemed to be a cold draught emanating from thin air. I now realised that the only way that any work would be done in the flat today would be if I were to stay with them and help complete it. They took a bit of persuading to stay, but eventually agreed, but only on the condition that I would stay there with them, and so Cyril departed to leave me to work with our two nervous workmen.

Things then became quite comical, as neither of these grown men would, in any way, be left alone; so, after wandering around like some kind of Siamese triplets we eventually found ourselves working together, all crammed into the main bathroom at the far end of the flat. Our tools, along with a box of Polyfiller which we had all been using, were on the floor, and after finishing my supply I went to mix some more, ... but the box, which had been there only minutes before, had vanished. I knew that no-one had left the room since we had all been together, so where the devil was it?

I decided to methodically go over the apartment, for by this time I was quite convinced that the flat had what I thought to be a poltergeist; so, beginning with the master-bedroom, which was at the far end of the flat, I started out on a thorough search for the missing box. I looked in the closets, in the drawers of all the furniture, and in any other hiding place where I thought the Polyfiller could possibly be - but with no luck. With Alf and Eddie stuck to me like flies we set off down the hall, past the bathroom we had been working in, and entered the next room - which was the kitchen. The kitchen was a good size, and had many fitted cupboards all the way around the walls; so with the bemused Alf and Eddie looking on I began opening doors. Starting to the left of the main door I worked my way around the room searching through the cupboards one by one, seeing all the normal things you would expect to find in any kitchen, until eventually, reaching the final one. This I opened to find, closed and neatly stacked along with tins of soup etc., the mysterious, missing box of filler.

The temperature seemed to drop, and then fell even further when I happened to look down the length of the hall to the small table upon which we had placed the wrapped whisky bottles. Things were certainly not as we had left them, for now one of the bottles had its paper half off; I asked Alf and Eddie if they had done it, although I was not aware that they had; they reacted quite angrily, accusing me of messing around. We headed down the hall, and upon reaching the table I noticed that something wasn't right as I looked into the drawing-room. Facing me was the oak drinks-cabinet with its door, once again, wide open. Now, none of us had been out of each other's sight, so it was obvious that it wasn't opened by any of us. I decided to take a closer look, with my two shadows in close attendance. I closed the door and locked it, and then tried to find if there was any possible way it could have opened itself; but the only way was to turn the key and to physically pull the door open.

We turned to leave the room, and were faced once again with the bottles of whisky, stood upon the hall table just outside, but things were not as we had last seen them here either. The half unwrapped bottle was now fully unwrapped and stood upon the wrapping paper, which had been flattened down as if by an iron, and was now spread out beneath both bottles. This had happened while our backs were turned for no more than one minute whilst in the drawing-room attending to the drinks cabinet.

Alf then exclaimed 'What the hell is that?'

Looking down the hall and on the floor there was Alf's tool box, inside which now stood a large wooden pick-axe handle! Well, that just about did it; both of the men were now really frightened, and I also felt quite disturbed, especially when noticing the drinks cabinet door was once again wide open. They again accused me of messing around, but knew quite well that it had been nothing to do with me, for I had not been out of their sight. This turned out to be the straw that broke the camel's back, and I now happily agreed with them that enough was surely enough, and decided that our day's work, or what we could do of it, had come to an end. I telephoned Cyril and told him we were leaving; I then telephoned Mr N at his office in Golden Square, Soho, and tried to explain something of what had been going on. He was very concerned and apologetic and asked if everyone was alright. He then proposed that, along with Cyril, we should meet at the flat the very next day, to which I agreed. So, with great relief we set about collecting our tools and equipment in order to get the hell out of there - or so we thought - for we were soon to find out that the flat had other plans, and was not going to let us out of its clutches that easily.

In order to leave the burglar alarm had to be set: this involved locking all doors, pressing the set-button on the system, which was inside a closet in the hall, locking the closet and finally leaving and locking the entrance door, all in a set time, but try as I might, the system refused to set; something was triggering one of the movement detectors in the dining-room (of the swinging chandelier). We went through this routine of checking and resetting for almost an hour, by which time Cyril, accompanied by my younger sister Karen (who could not resist a good haunting), had arrived. He immediately took control and insisted upon being locked in the closet with the alarm system. This game continued for a further half an hour, and then, for some unexplained reason, at 3 p.m. on the dot, it finally set - and released us. So off we all went feeling dazed and confused, but a whole lot better to be out of there. The whole thing, though disturbing, was not malicious; in fact, it seemed as if something had been toying with us, and had certainly succeeded in getting our attention.

The following day we met Mr N back at Cadogan Place. He was still very concerned, and asked us repeatedly if we were all OK and had not been affected too badly by our experience. Having reassured him that we were all fine, and made of quite tough stuff, we sat down to discuss the rather queer business at hand. He told us about the many strange happenings of the last few months in this once happy and peaceful home. It had started quite suddenly with the damage to the various pieces of furniture around the flat which, over a short period of time, had increased dramatically in frequency. No-one was ever seen to do it, but the discarded tools and their damage would always be there on returning home. This was to prompt them to install the sophisticated burglar alarm-system, which had given us so much trouble. All this expense was to no avail: the incidents continued, and now progressed to include the consumption of whisky. Mr N went on to tell us that on several occasions upon their return, they had found upon the drawing-room table an ever-diminishing bottle of whisky, which was always accompanied by two used and empty glasses. It would seem that we now had a case of spirits consuming spirits ... which must be quite unusual, and was something I had never come across before. He then confided that although the events that had happened to us had been quite disturbing, he was also greatly relieved, for he had believed it was possible, even though unlikely, that Mrs N may in some way have been the responsible party and could possibly have been suffering some kind of nervous breakdown. This was now out of the question, being confirmed by all of our experiences of the previous day.

We then discussed what actually could be going on, to eventually reach the only possible conclusion that this had to be something of a paranormal nature; and though we were quite adept at fixing most things this was way beyond our expertise. I suggested that he make enquiries through the local church into the possibility of having the flat exorcised or blessed, believing this to be a good idea, and in reality the only available option. ... So, Mr N then set about making the necessary enquiries.

Some weeks later Mr N called and spoke to Cyril. He informed him that a priest would be coming to Cadogan Place to carry out an exorcism, and at the request of the priest, a Father Dominique, Alf, Eddie and myself should be there to meet him, as he would like to discuss with all the people involved exactly what had happened. On the day of the appointment we set off once again for Cadogan Place, with the reluctant and still nervous Alf and Eddie in tow.

Mr N welcomed us, and we sat in the drawing-room talking about the strangeness of the morning's journey that we were about to embark upon. We were soon joined by Father Dominique who, far from being the wizened old priest which I think we had all expected, turned out to be a tall, handsome man, not unlike the actor Christopher Reeve, but instead of a Superman outfit he was wearing the full-length cassock of a Dominican priest. We were all introduced, and one by one related to him in our own words what had happened upon that most strange of days. Having heard our stories he then informed us that this was not poltergeist activity, of which he had had much experience, but was instead a full-blown haunting, where a disturbed and trapped spirit was carrying out these disturbing acts. He then revealed that in the Parish records he had found the probable cause.

Nearly a century before the building, which at that time had not yet been broken up into apartments, was owned by an artist who happened to be a homosexual. His lover, a carpenter by trade, murdered him there and then went on to hang himself. We were all stunned - this was just like a movie, and even looked like one with Father Dominique in his attire who then, picking up his case, proceeded to the serious business of the day. He opened the small leather case to take out his sash and a few other adornments, and commenced to dress himself for the appointed task. We set off around the flat, led by the exorcist, who held a bible in one hand and a small vial of holy water in the other, speaking loudly the Latin words of the exorcism, whilst sprinkling the holy water in blessing throughout the flat. It was quite an experience.

Returning once more to the drawing-room, his work now done for the day, he removed his garments, put them back in the case, and we sat to talk over a welcome cup of coffee. He was a fascinating man, and told us many stories of the strange things that he had had to deal with as part of his most unusual job. Pointing to a scar above his left eye, he revealed that this had been received when attending a family whose home had become plagued by strange events. Furniture was being rearranged, pictures moved, and the kitchen, which appeared to be the centre of the disturbances, was in a constant form of disarray, with all the food being invisibly removed from the cupboards and strewn around the floor; and the kitchen chairs often being stacked into bizarre towers. Upon his arrival Father Dominique had been welcomed into the hall, and had immediately been struck by a can of baked beans, which had flown from the empty kitchen to strike him in the eye, cutting him and requiring several stitches. This, he told us, was a poltergeist, which had been caused by the disturbed mental state of the teenage son, whose pent-up energy would suddenly be released, resulting in the movement of the many objects.

He then went on to tell us about a Russian friend of his, whose speciality was his ability to move objects with the power of his mind, or telekinesis, as it is known. When travelling together around London in his car he revealed to us that he never had to pay for parking, for his Russian friend was able to move the arm inside the parking meter by just holding his finger near it. Of course, he realised that this was dishonest, but assured us that he said his required number of 'Hail Marys' in penance. After he had entertained us with his fascinating stories we said our goodbyes, and after what had been a most unusual and very interesting day, left Cadogan Place for what turned out to be the very last time.

You are probably wondering if the exorcism was successful: well, I can't really answer that for certain, for we were never to see Mr and Mrs N again. They never returned to the flat, and went off to live we know not where, choosing to leave us, as well as these particular experiences, in the past. I am sure they were only too happy to put this strange and disturbing time behind them, and I will always remember them both most fondly. But this story was not quite over yet, for Cadogan Place still had one last surprise up its sleeve.

Around two years later, whilst flat-hunting with my girlfriend at the time in the Portobello Road area of West London, we viewed a flat. My girlfriend had always had a fascination with ghosts, and at every flat we viewed she would ask the owner whether it was haunted, to which the usual answer was 'no', - but on this one occasion the man who, like my girlfriend also happened to be Canadian, replied, 'This flat isn't, but the one I used to live in sure was'.

We asked him what had happened. He then told us of almost

identical experiences such as we had had at Cadogan Place: damaged furniture, etc.

I asked him, 'Where was the flat?'

His reply made me shudder ... for not only was it Cadogan Place once again, but this time, it was the house right next door.

CHAPTER THIRTEEN

FAMOUS PLACES FAMOUS FACES

*We are all in the gutter,
but some of us are looking at the stars.*
-Oscar Wilde.

I was most fortunate to have been born, and then to have grown up, in Chelsea, the magnetic hub of so many interesting people and places; but I was double-blessed to have, at the helm of my young life, a character such as my father Cyril, without whom so many doors would have remained firmly locked, and their interesting contents therefore inaccessible.

For a short period of time, at the height of the Swinging Sixties, living in Chelsea was almost like being an extra in a life-sized film-set, for as you wandered the streets it was not unusual to pass Dracula, or Christopher Lee, out shopping in broad daylight seemingly unaffected by the light of the sun; or his counterpart in horror, the original Frankenstein, or Boris Karloff, walking quite safely with no sign of a pursuing mob (who were now more likely to be seen in pursuit of the common, but necessarily fleeing shapes, of the Fab Four). Lawrence of Arabia, or Peter O Toole, along with his friend and sometime drinking partner, Richard Harris, would be seen in their usual watering-holes, filling up with great regularity, for as they say, 'A man's not a camel'. Dr Strangelove, or Peter Sellers, was always flying around the streets in his black Mini Cooper S, accompanied on occasion by the sexy Swedish seductress Britt Ekland. The pink convertible E-Type Jaguar of porn star, Fiona Richmond, was also often seen: this had been a parting gift from her lover, the West End club owner, Paul Raymond, who had added its memorable personalised number plate bearing the message, FU2 - surely making it one of the most generous and memorable last words of all time! John Lennon's psychedelic Rolls cruised the streets, while Diana Dors' huge pink Cadillac would be seen floating, as only large American cars can do, up and down the Kings Road, passing many more famous faces as it went.

The Kings Road was the catwalk where over the years I spotted both Sinatras - Nancy and Frank - strutting their stuff; but the biggest 'strut' of them all had to be the afternoon that fellow brat-packer, Sammy Davis Junior, did his thing in his own inimitable way. I was sat with friends outside Picasso, the Italian restaurant-bar, drinking cappuccinos when, from far off along the crowded pavement and heading our way, came the sound of blaring music. As it eventually reached our spot there appeared the writhing form of Sammy, decked out in flowery hippie clothing, beads and bells, and with what was the first ghetto-blaster we had ever seen perched up on his shoulder. He swept past, and blasted his way off along the Kings Road, to eventually disappear into the purple haze left behind by the coolest cat of them all - the one and only Jimi Hendrix. The Rolling Stones were also seen around quite a lot, for, like the Beatles, they all had homes in Chelsea at this time; these were nothing like their shabby dump of so few years ago when they had lived in the Worlds End, for now they were more likely to be seen coming and going from prestigious homes in the likes of Cheyne Walk, no longer just Rolling Stones, but now also rolling in money - the boys had done really well. Twiggy, Brigitte Bardot, Jean Shrimpton, Jane Asher, Catherine Deneuve, Julie Christie and the ever-faithful Marianne, were just some of the pretty faces that decorated our streets in this golden period. They just don't make them like that anymore.

Just around the corner is Upper Cheyne Walk where, one day, working along with several of Cyril's men, a visitor was to call upon our client, a Mrs Scarr, who would make it clear in no uncertain terms that one should never judge a book by its cover. We were decorating the common parts of this large house - the lobby, entrance hall, staircase and landings - so the men were spread all around when, just before lunch-time, the doorbell rang. I looked down from the upstairs landing to watch one of the men, a chap called Bill, open the door, and after muttering something the door was then slammed quite firmly in the face of the caller. Bill then called up to me, 'There's an old tramp outside who wants to see Mrs Scarr'.

I set off to find the lady, and informed her that there was someone at the door who wished to see her. As I watched from above, she opened the door and said, while flinging her arms around the mystery guest, 'Paul darling, how wonderful to see you! Do come in'.

In walked a shabbily dressed old man in a tatty grey overcoat, looking for all the world like he had indeed spent the night on a park bench. But appearances can be deceiving, for as I looked closer I realised that this was no ordinary tramp, but was, in fact, one of the richest and meanest men in the world, a man so mean that guests to Sutton Place, his Surrey mansion, who needed to make a phone call, would have to use a payphone. It was none other than Paul Getty himself, and waiting outside for him was his black chauffeur, alongside his old and equally tatty, huge black Cadillac.

During lunch we had a good laugh about Bill's case of mistaken identity, of which he was rather proud, for Bill, being a fully paid-up union man and a staunch socialist, had really enjoyed being the one who had slammed the door in the face of one of the world's great capitalists.

When I was about seven or eight, Cyril took me to meet another of his many clients, one that he knew I would be more than interested to meet. After ringing the door-bell of the house in Chesham Place, you can imagine my delight as it was opened by none other than Richard Green, known to us all at the time on the TV as the good-guy-outlaw, Robin Hood. He was a handsome and gentle man, and, with his deep distinctive voice, he welcomed us in to his hide-out; for strangely, this is exactly what his home had become. Inside, he had his own personal cinema, where he spent most of his days; he would sit alone, watching endless re-runs of the many films that he had starred in during his heyday. It was really rather sad, and one could only hope that one day his band of merry men may come to his rescue.

Chelsea, being situated as it is in London, is not a place where you would expect to find a stately home, but it did have its very own self-professed stately homo - the naked civil servant himself: the flamboyant Quentin Crisp. Many a bus ride was enlivened by his gay wit and colourful presence as he came and went, with his ever-changing shade of purple hair, from his boudoir in Beaufort Street. Strangely, almost a century before, Beaufort Street also happened to be the home of Lady Wilde, the mother of that other famous London dandy, Oscar; he would often visit her there, attracting, just like his gay counterpart Quentin so many years later, a great deal of attention.

Over the years, we were to work in many lovely parts of Chelsea, but my favourite of them all had to be the Boltons. These huge Regency-style houses run in an oval shape around the central core, inside which stands the Parish Church of Saint Mary with its lovely spire, surrounded by gardens; all in all a most desirable place to live, and indeed, also not a bad place to work. One particular job there would give us the opportunity to meet one of the silver-screen's greatest icons, for the house involved was owned by the daughter of none other than 'Lily of The Lamplight' herself, Marlene Dietrich. One day her daughter informed us that her mother would be paying us a visit. This naturally caused a lot of excitement among our workmen who were, on the whole, of her generation. When the doorbell rang all eyes gazed expectantly across the large entrance hall which, incidentally, contained a grand piano, to watch her hoped-for, even grander, entrance. Our, but more importantly, Marlene's, big moment had come. Marlene, being rather vain, was very keen on making a grand entrance; but things, as you will soon hear, were not to go quite the way that she had hoped for.

The door was opened by the daughter, and her mother, the unmistakeable and iconic figure, swept into the hall, wearing a large hat, with her long dark outfit flowing behind her. She had only made it a few steps when Cyril's brother, my Uncle Fred, sat himself down at the piano, and said to the now fast approaching Prima Donna, 'You sing it and I'll play it!'

The brakes were applied, and with a look that would have killed most men (but not Uncle Fred), she turned around and swept out from the house, without having said a single word, let alone sung a song. It was a great disappointment for us all, but was also quite typical of this rather difficult star.

Another interesting job in the Boltons would find us working this time in not one but two of these glorious houses. They were both owned by one man, for being a Saudi Prince he was in the position to have just about anything that money can buy. This was something that we were to witness with the constant stream of deliveries to the house, and on one occasion, this being the birthday of his ten year old son, we watched with great interest as a wooden crate, at least 10 ft long, was carried up the steps into one of the huge reception rooms; what on earth could it be? Later that day we had our answer, as now, assembled and standing in the centre of the room, was a one-third-scale, remote-control helicopter ... an incredible gift for a small boy who, by now (this being some years on), will undoubtedly have more than one full-sized version as well.

This particular house was more like a hotel than a home, for it was used for all the entertaining and general day-to-day business of this wealthy and busy man. The entire basement, which was of a considerable size, was one huge kitchen where the ten or so staff, all Arab and wearing white djellabas, would work almost endlessly, preparing and cooking huge banquets for the many inmates and visitors of both houses. One old man would sit all day with vast bowls of rice between his legs, his job being to sort it and pick out any impurities; while another would, with some help, prepare the meats, which at times would be an entire goat: this would be stuffed with many kinds of vegetables, herbs and spices and then placed inside one of the huge ovens to roast all day. We were always offered food from the vast kitchen, so at lunchtime we were able to indulge in some of the wonderful Arab recipes that were created there - and boy, were they good.

The largest rooms were on the ground and first floors, and these were used for socialising and dining. They were filled, as you would expect, with expensive and richly-coloured furniture, all with more than a little gold embellishment which was to be found in most of the fabrics and decoration, and is much favoured by the Arabs. All of the upper-floors were taken up with the accommodation for the huge numbers of staff, where some of the many rooms were literally wall-to-wall beds with not a gap between them.

One day, I met the House Manager carrying an attaché case on his way down the steps at the front of the house. I said, 'Good morning, going anywhere nice?'

He replied, 'No, I am just going shopping to buy a couple of cars.' - at which point he opened the attaché case to reveal the obvious contents (being Arabs it could only be one thing) - which was wall-to-wall fifty pound notes. Later that day he returned, along with the latest toys: a brand new Bentley, which was closely followed by a brand new Aston Martin – boy, does money talk ...

In our time there we had all noticed that something was missing from the first house, this being not a single sighting of any members of the fairer sex. It turned out that this particular household was a totally male desert; but the women had to be somewhere, for these were, after all, Arab men.

Everything became clear one day when we got to work in the second house, a house I had always longed to visit, for it had once been the London home of film stars and renowned party-givers, Douglas Fairbanks and Mary Pickford, whose home in Hollywood was known as Pickfair. We were escorted to the house by the House Manager, who showed us to the room which we were to decorate. He then informed us that we were not to leave the room without an escort, as this was the home of the Saudi Prince's many wives, or his harem. On one occasion, whilst leaving the house, we were presented with what at first could easily be mistaken for a mirage or, at least, a scene from The Arabian Nights. We were stopped by two huge, dark-skinned guards who were dressed in full Arab ceremonial costume, curved sabres and all. We were then herded into a corner, as a train of traditionally-dressed Arab ladies scampered past, their beautiful, many-coloured silk dresses flowing behind them; the air was thick with the smell of expensive perfume, and the tinkle of even more expensive jewellery, all accompanied by their giggles as they passed, to peek at us over their yashmaks. Off they went, giggling away, as gangs of girls will do the whole world over, to disappear, like the genie into his bottle, into the room which was the Prince's own personal oasis. With the girls back once more inside the safety of their room, we were allowed to pass their door, outside which the eunuch guards now stood, their sabres drawn across their chests, to stand guard over the Prince's precious harem. It was hard to believe that we were still in 1980s London.

Inevitably, Cyril would find himself working in London's clubland, and, as ever, it was not to be any old club, but the oldest Boys' Club of them all - the very private and exclusive Whites, in St James. For over three centuries this has been the place where many of the most influential, and, of course, wealthy characters of British history, have whiled away their time; but their policy of exclusivity would for some strange reason leave even the great Sir Winston Churchill outside the famous black doors.

Our first visit to Whites was in the early 1970s, and we were given the tour around what were a collection of grand, but very tired and dowdy rooms, by the then Club Secretary, Mr West. The entrance hall contained an old-fashioned telephone booth and a large glass-fronted reception area, inside which were found the hall-porters, their job being to welcome the welcome, and keep out the unwelcome. They would also arrange the mail in the members' personal cubby-holes which lined the back wall; this was along with their other duty of working the switchboard, which acted as a discrete buffer between the members and the outside world. Behind this was a room, filled just like most of the ground-floor rooms, with large leather armchairs and many tables, and upon the walls hung many small portraits of some of the club's famous past members. Moving further in we entered the large hall with the cloakrooms off to the left, the grand double-staircase on the right, and at the end was the bar where, upon the wall a naked gas flame burned, that over the years must have lit many of the cigars that had stained the once white walls to the colour of coffee. Beyond this, at the very back of the building, was the galleried, glass-ceilinged billiard-room, again, filled with many ancient leather sofas and armchairs.

Cyril and Mr West were getting on famously as we proceeded up the grand staircase to view the card-room: this we were to decorate some years later in preparation for the stag-night of Prince Charles before his marriage to Lady Di. We then entered the largest room in Whites, the dining- or morning-room, as it is known. This high room with its fine, painted, panelled ceiling and ornate cornice, was to be the place that we were to decorate - if we passed inspection. This, as it now turned out, was to become more or less a formality, as from the far end of the room entered the familiar figure of Major Desmond Fitzgerald, who was not only one of our oldest clients, but much to our surprise, also happened to be the club's Chairman who, upon recognising us, remarked, 'Hello Cyril, I knew that you would find your way here one day.'

From that moment we were to become the club's decorators for many years, which would require us to devote all of our resources to it for the whole month of August, this being the time that the club closed for its summer break.

We continued the tour, taking in the smaller rooms, and then proceeded upstairs to the second floor to the main kitchen: this was serviced by a dumb-waiter which ran from the basement, allowing the delivery of supplies upward, and also passed through a small service-room at the back of the morning-room from which the food could be collected by the waiters. We eventually reached the upper floors of this large old building, which contained many small rooms which were occupied by the jumbled collection of live-in staff, many of whom had been at Whites for most of their lives. The whole place was really quite fascinating, for all around us were many different periods of the past, all stitched carefully together to create a time of its own from which the present, just like poor old Winston, had been most definitely denied entrance.

All work carried out in Whites had first to be approved by the club's committee who, being on the whole gentlemen of advanced years, would put up stiff resistance to almost any proposed changes to their familiar and private world; but after any of our works had been carried out were always most generous with their approval. Last of all, we were taken down to the basement, which contained the obvious wine cellar, the coal cellar and the club storerooms, where all the spare parts and bric-a-brac of many years were piled high upon many shelves, giving it the appearance of a rather specialised and interesting hardware store; this was run very efficiently by the club's old caretaker, Frank, who was the only person that could find anything in this, his own world within worlds. Starting with the morning-room, which required the well-worn 19th-century deep red, flock wallpaper to be reproduced (as it was no longer manufactured, and the members naturally insisted upon it remaining the same), we were, over the years, to redecorate almost all of Whites, both inside and out, and, as with most of our work, Cyril and all the men enjoyed it enormously.

Of all the famous faces that I was to meet over the years my favourite couple who, again because of Cyril, I had been fortunate to know, had to be the Profumos, or Mr and Mrs P, as we called them.

John Profumo, even to this day, nearly fifty years on, is only ever remembered for the minor indiscretion he committed when caught in the nasty political web, spun by who knows who, into which he had so unwisely fallen. This was most unfortunate for us all, for he was, as the rest of his life was to prove, a truly good man, and this one mistake was to cost him his political career. Fortunately, it was not to cost him the love and support of his wife, the lovely Mrs P, or Valerie Hobson, as she is known from her many roles in films and stage who, during this most difficult period, with all the ghouls of Fleet Street tearing into him, stood unwaveringly by his side. Mr P was to devote the rest of his life to charitable work for the support of underprivileged children - a far cry from the likes of Tony Blair who, against most peoples wishes, not only involved us in a war, but is as we speak engaged in various financially rewarding Tony projects all over the world. 'By their deeds they shall be known'.

One summer day, during a visit to their lovely Chelsea mews house, Mrs P, noticing that I was not my normal self (for I was suffering from, and shrouded by, a wall of depression) took me aside, leaving Cyril and Mr P to talk shop, in order to give me a much needed pep-talk. She was most gracious and understanding, offering me her hand of support, and stating wisely that she knew that I had the love and help of my parents, but that at times they could be too close, and someone more removed was sometimes needed to see our problems clearly. She was absolutely right, and after a real heart-to-heart talk, she told me to call on her at any time when in need, or, if I would rather speak man-to-man, Jack (Mr P), would be only too glad to help. This small act of kindness was typical of them, and although it could not cure my depression, it certainly raised my spirits enough to enable me to look once more beyond the wall.

Some months later, during a search through a pile of old records in my brother-in-law, Ray's, Chelsea junk shop, I was delighted to come across a 78 rpm copy of 'I Whistle a Happy Tune' from the stage show of *The King and I*, sung by no other than Mrs P herself, in her other role of Valerie Hobson. Having bought the record I informed Cyril that I would like to present it to Mrs P as a surprise, and as luck would have it he told me that he was meeting Mrs P at the home of their good friend, Lady McIndoe, in a few days' time; so the plan was hatched. On Thursday afternoon I set off, along with my best mate Jon Hughes, or Squatter, as I had nicknamed him some years before, for our appointment with Mrs P. Upon arriving, I presented her with the old 78. She looked it over, and then, with a huge smile on her face, said, 'Where on earth did you find this? I've not seen one of these for many years.'

She thanked me, gave me a huge hug, and then, assuming her role, commanded us to take a seat. With her small audience gathered, she straightened up, clasped her hands in front of her, and went off into what was to be our own personal performance of the song from her role in *The King and I* of so many years before. This tall, mature, but still very attractive lady, sang, danced and pranced all around the room, putting on quite a show - it was wonderful, and something I shall always treasure. After more thankyous from Mrs P we said our goodbyes, and left Cyril, as usual, to have a drink in the good company of his lady-friends. Whistling a happy tune we made our way around the corner to Picasso in the Kings Road where we sat outside, drinking yet another cappuccino, to watch, and do some more whistling of another kind, as all the pretty girls walked by.

The fabulous collection of shops that made up the Kings Road of the Swinging Sixties were such a treat to have close by, as unlike today where most high streets are homogenised versions of each other, nearly all of the shops then were privately owned, quite unique and completely original. For a few short years the Kings Road would be stuck in an eternal spring, with new shops opening and blossoming almost daily, all vying to outdo each other with evermore way-out creations. They were formed with the creative juices of the new generation, who found it relatively easy to rent shops at this time - even in such a great location as the Kings Road; for most of it was owned by The Church of England, and rents were cheap and so the risks were small.

Apart from the obvious boutiques like Bazaar or John Stephen, which were the first to appear, there would be added many more, like the wonderful Stop the Shop, with its circular rotating floor: this gave it an ever-changing window display which, of course, all the customers were part of. Just across the road was the crazy and colourful Mr Freedom, with its collection of wild multi-coloured dungarees and Marvel Comic-inspired baseball shirts. Next door was, what I believe to have been the first American-style hamburger bar. This was called Orange Julius, after their delicious drink of the same name, which was a glass of freshly-squeezed orange juice into which was blended an egg - it may well have been the first smoothie. There was Top Gear with its bullseye entrance; Quorum, which sold the wonderful creations of Ossie Clarke and Celia Birtwell; Antiquarius, where you could find all sorts of quirky items; there was Lord Kitchener's Valet, which specialised in old military-style clothes, as worn by the Beatles in their Sergeant Pepper period; but the best of them all was, I believe, the wonderfully named Granny Takes A Trip, or Grannies, as it was known, and which also just happened to be, where else, but in the good old Worlds End.

One sunny afternoon, during the Summer of Love (1967), the jungle-line of the Worlds End carried the exciting news that the Beatles were in Grannies. In no time at all the shop, which was up a few steps from the road, had its door securely locked, as it was besieged by crowds of fans all eager to see, or even get a piece of, their idols. After a short while a chauffeur-driven Rolls (not John's psychedelic one), pulled up outside. Grannies door opened, and out ran Paul McCartney accompanied by Keith Richards. They fought their way through the frenzied crowd and eventually reached the safety of the waiting Rolls, which then took off like greased lightning, leaving behind many screaming and crying girls, some of whom fell to their knees to kiss the pavement where their idols had just trod.

The first boutique that I remember that was solely dedicated to the sale of jeans and all things denim, was Jean Machine which, by creating its own brand called UFO, would break the monopoly held by the three established brands: Levis, Wranglers and Lee Coopers. These were only available from shops that sold work clothing, this being the original purpose of the tough and durable denim before it became the popular fashion item that we all know so well. Owning a pair of Levis was quite an undertaking and involved some very strange rituals. You had first to buy them a size too big, as they were not pre-shrunk in those days, and shrinking them was usually done whilst wearing them in the bath: this was something that, because of the high indigo content, always left your legs a most unattractive shade of blue. Having now got them to fit, much time would be spent perfecting them, which involved some very odd behaviour. Some of this involved swimming in the sea with them on, much washing, and even rubbing cigarette ash into them, for it was believed that the saltpetre in the ash would help to bring them to their much-desired colour, which was the most wonderful shade of turquoisey blue, and yes, it's true, that Levis when new were so thick they did stand up on their own.

The Worlds End was also the venue for one of the first shops dedicated to the sale of stripped-pine furniture. It was called, appropriately, Sophistocat, for among the tables and wardrobes there roamed what has to be the most effective burglar deterrent ever - a lion called Christian. He had been bought as a cub from another Chelsea institution, the department store Harrods, and could often be seen riding around in the back of cars, or even being walked upon a leash up and down Slaidburn Street, where he did his very large toilet, much to the confusion and dismay of the many cats and dogs whose rank in the pecking-order had been so drastically reduced.

All these interesting places would, of course, attract a great many famous faces, and there was no better place to observe them all than from a much sought-after seat on the pavement outside Piccaso, the funky old Italian cafe-bar, which sat right in the hub of it all. Incredible as it now seems with the Kings Road awash in cappuccino bars, Piccaso was then the only place in the whole of Chelsea where a cappuccino could be had, and, needless to say, many an afternoon was spent sat there drinking them, whilst watching the crazy and colourful world of the swinging sixties and the punky seventies go by.

Pubs were also a major part of the life of the Kings Road, and at this time there were almost too many to count. The Man in the Moon, the Markham Arms, the Trafalgar, with its dance floor; the Chelsea Potter, the Lord Nelson, the Six Bells, the Bird's Nest and the wonderful stainless-steel-clad Chelsea Drugstore, were just a few of the watering-holes that were popular at the time. Friday night was always Drugstore night where, in the upstairs bar, Mark the DJ would spin the latest discs, accompanied by Denise, the delectable, scantily-clad Go-Go girl, shaking her stuff in a raised cage by his side. There were the inevitable lock-ins, for pubs were only licensed until 11 p.m., and on many occasions you would find an assortment of plain-clothes Chelsea policemen alongside Chelsea footballers, chucking back Bacardi and Coke well into the wee hours of the morning, and all before their big games on Saturday afternoon - no wonder they struggled!

Sadly, today most of the pubs are just memories, with the Drugstore being used as an outlet for the ghastly Macdonalds, the Lord Nelson as a Building society, and the Man in the Moon is now a restaurant. Even the funky Pheasantry, once home to the likes of Augustus John, Annigoni, Germain Greer and Eric Clapton, to name but a few, is now a Pizza Express. Their passing, as with many of the colourful boutiques has, sadly, left the Kings Road a mere shadow of its former self.

Life in London was not all love and light: it also had its dark underbelly. The bright lights of Chelsea would quite naturally attract their fair share of villains, wide-boys and even murderers. The Krays and the Richardsons were two of the toughest of the London gangs and were often seen around the Kings Road, their Jags, the chosen transport of the London villain, taking them to some pub or restaurant, or more likely, to a casino club such as the popular Cromwellian at South Kensington, where they could indulge their gambling habits. There they would meet up with local villains, such as the sometime intimate friend of Princess Margaret, John Bindon.

John, like most villains, loved to tell his stories, most of which would include a large number of girls and of course just a little violence. He was a natural story-teller so he made very easy listening, and whether talking about his tough London life or his adventures travelling the world as a minder with the rock group Led Zeppelin, he was always entertaining. His eventual death from aids must raise questions about the sad end of Princess Margaret herself, as she remains to this day the only member of the immediate Royal Family to have foregone the usual procedure of burial, choosing instead, rather suspiciously, to be cremated. Bindon never revealed what went on with the Princess, but was always keen to tell when he had been summoned to her side, and the twinkle in his eye told all that needed to be known.

The London villains were a complex mix of characters, sometimes entertaining, sometimes funny, but always unpredictably dangerous, and because of this were really best avoided when possible. They were always highly visible with their flash cars, suits and confident swagger, all designed to make them stand out, and leaving you in no doubt of who and what they were.

This was not to be the case with one evil character who was to cross Cyril's path right at the beginning of his working life; for this one was not looking for attention ... he was a real wolf in sheep's clothing. John George Haigh is now well known in British criminal law as one of the most notorious serial-killers of all time, his ghastly crimes earning him the unsavoury title of the Acid Bath Murderer.

At the end of the Second World War the young Cyril was to go to work as a decorator at number 79 Gloucester Road. There he would meet the small, moustached, middle-class owner, who put him to work decorating various parts of the house. Cyril, as was customary then for tradesmen, entered the house through the basement, and was immediately struck by the most appalling smell which permeated the whole place. Added to this, he noticed that stored around the basement were many large steel drums, and that the large butler-sink, in which he had to wash his brushes, was missing all of its enamel. Over the ensuing weeks, never being one to shirk a challenge, he set about using every trick in the book to rid the place of its terrible odour, but after exhausting his formidable arsenal of detergents and bleach he had to admit defeat, and by now, having completed his work, left the still badly smelling house for the last time.

Shortly after, having prepared his bill, Cyril was due to return to 79 Gloucester Road in order to meet Haigh to receive payment for his work, but being unwell and in need of the money, the appointment was kept instead by my mother, Joyce, who out of necessity would take along with her my eldest sister Pauline, who was still a baby. Joyce thankfully returned home. She was safe but badly shaken and raged at Cyril, 'How could you let me go there, and with Pauline! That man is evil! The whole place stank of evil!'

They had all had a lucky escape, and this was an experience they were never likely to forget. Even though it would be several years before Haigh was caught, my mother's instincts were, as ever, completely right, as he was found to have killed six to nine people with at least three of them being murdered and then dissolved in acid in the basement of Gloucester Road. After a trial in which he was prosecuted by Sir Hartley Shawcross (who, coincidentally, some years later was to become a client of Cyril's), Haigh would be deservedly hanged by the public executioner, Albert Pierrepoint, in Wandsworth prison in 1949.

Many years later Cyril was to tell this story to the 6th form girls of Hurlingham School in West London who were at the time involved in a project based around London's notorious murderers. Needless to say, Cyril revelled in all the attention he got and gave the girls a wonderful time as he relived the lucky escape he and his family had had from the clutches of the Acid Bath Murderer.

CHAPTER FOURTEEN

RIGHT ON THE NOSE

There is nothing so difficult to marry as a large nose.
-Oscar Wilde

Cyril, being a big man, loved his food, and would find many ways whilst out and about in various parts of London to satisfy his, and it must be said, my appetite, and right at the top of our list just had to be that once staple diet of all true Londoners, pie and mash. Pie and mash shops were once common all over London and within their sparklingly clean, tiled interiors you could eat not only well but also very cheaply. There was always a queue, and apart from those eating inside, many people would buy to take away, using their own various sized containers into which the whole meal was put. Along with the pies and the mash there was also liquer, a green sauce or gravy made from parsley, and the water from that other key requirement of a good pie and mash shop, stewed eels - all in all a substantial meal. The pies were baked on trays in batches of sixteen or so and standing in the queue was always frustrating, as, with our mouths watering, before our very eyes tray after tray of piping hot pies would quickly disappear. Eventually our turn would come, and so the double-pie, double-mash, double-eels and liquor would be squeezed onto a plate, and once seated we would tuck in with great gusto, to finish it all off with that other great requisite of Londoners, a good old cup of tea.

So popular was this dish with our family that we even found time to have it as a take-away on my sister Pauline's wedding day, after which we set off with bulging stomachs (which attracted some suspicious looks at the bride) for Chelsea Old Church, to somehow make it through the long ceremony

Cyril's other great love was the food hall in Harrods which, just like his beloved pie and mash shops, also has a tiled interior, but this being Harrods would of course mean that the tiles are somewhat more elaborate; in fact they are quite beautiful. Wandering through this glorious food emporium with Cyril was always guaranteed to be fun for he loved trying new things, so apart from his usual purchase of sausages, saveloys, various pork pies, hams, tongue and all sorts of cheese, we would always return home with any number of new and untried delights to which my mother would always remark, 'What on earth have you bought now?' Last but not least there were the cafés.

Owning and running cafés seems to be a family tradition, having had at one time or another, an aunt and two sisters who have been involved in the great tradition of feeding the insatiable appetite of London's workers. During the 1980s my sister Sue ran such a place in Burnaby Street, Chelsea, and, just like most of these cafés, it would attract a great variety of different characters, being in some ways a kind of early morning pub, or, indeed, somewhere to recover from the previous night in an actual pub. Quite often Cyril and I, when at a loose end, would pop into Sue's cafe for a hearty breakfast and a good yak - something that comes quite naturally to most Londoners, who certainly know how to rabbit. One morning, having ordered our traditional double-bubble, egg, bacon and beans, we were joined at our table by one of the local characters, a chap called Ken Seely.

Ken was a short, stocky Irishman, who at the time was in his mid-fifties. He worked in the local Lots Road Power Station as a night-watchman. The old power station supplied the electricity which ran the London Underground; this meant that it was working round the clock, and so, just like many of London's food markets - Covent Garden and Billingsgate to name but two with equally unsociable working hours, its workers, in compensation, had their own all-night Pubs. Licencing laws at the time were pretty archaic, with opening hours from 11a.m. through to 3 p.m. at which point they would close, only to reopen two and a half hours later at 5.30 p.m. with the final session ending at 11p.m. So, Ken with his unorthodox working hours was never short of a drink, with the appropriately named Balloon public house a few short steps away across Lots Road.

He had come to London as a boy, and earned his keep by bare-fist prize-fighting at many fairs, or even on the back-streets of old London. This brutal occupation involved taking on all-comers, who were given a set time to last in the ring against him ... not much of a job. As you would expect, his face and body took quite a lot of punishment for a good many years, and he was eventually required to stop.

The worst of the damage from all the years of fighting had been done to his nose, which really was a most unpleasant sight; this was also added to by his typically Irish love for booze, and their combined effects had left his nose distorted and swollen, clustered with lumps and veins, resembling more an oversize strawberry than the nose it had obviously once been. So there we sat, chatting away, trying our best not to look at the ghastly protuberance facing us across the table, but this was easier said than done, for no matter how hard you tried your eyes were always pulled back as if by a magnet. After a little while, our breakfast arrived; Cyril looked at the food, gulped, and then looked at Ken's nose and gulped again. He put down his knife and fork, and with the look of a man with a bad taste in his mouth said to Ken, 'I'm sorry Ken, but your nose is putting me off my breakfast. Would you mind sitting at another table.'

There was a shocked silence, and Ken, with eyes now filled with tears, said, 'I'm sorry Cyril', he stood up and with his shoulders slumped he moved off, to sit down with his back to us at a table across the room. Now, Cyril had not quite finished with Ken. Having finished his breakfast, he walked over to his table and sat down to face him and his offending nose.

He said, 'Sorry about that Ken, but you really ought to do something about that nose. I'll tell you what to do. Go and see your doctor, tell him that you can't live with your nose like that any more because people are making fun of you, and your life has become so miserable that you want to kill yourself. If you do that, they'll have to sort it out for you'.

Ken, having registered what Cyril had just said to him, was again almost brought to tears. He thanked Cyril, and told him he was the first person ever to be honest with him about his nose, and asked if the doctors could really help him. Cyril assured him that they could, and probably would, if he did exactly what he had told him.

Some weeks later we again found ourselves in Sue's cafe, when in walked Ken. He made a strange sight indeed for his nose this time was even larger than before, but this was due to a massive bandage, which covered it, and, fortunately for everyone there, concealed the offending protuberance. He homed straight in on Cyril and said, 'It worked Cyril!' and thanked him over and over again.

When the bandages eventually came off Ken had got a new nose and a new spring in his step, and he never failed to thank Cyril whenever they met. Honesty is sometimes the right policy, and in this particular case Cyril had hit the problem 'right on the nose'.

Whilst on the subject of noses, it reminds me of another story involving Cyril and my mother, Joyce. Relationships are never easy things to navigate smoothly, and it's not surprising that with all the pressures of life, including the added responsibility of having a large brood of children, that occasionally things could get a little heated. Well, such was the case, when one night in the middle of a row my mother was to be caught in the eye by Cyril's elbow. Her reaction was swift indeed, for she grabbed the nearest item to her, which happened to be a wooden hairbrush, and cracked Cyril right on the bridge of his nose, bringing immediate tears to his eyes. They of course made up, but the damage had already been done as they were to find out the very next morning, for between them they shared not just two lovely black eyes, as in the old song, but had gone one better to share three - one for Joyce and two for Cyril. They both loved telling this story, and it always got a good laugh, though it must be said that Cyril's eyes always watered just a little with its telling.

Cyril retired from work in 1985, though being the social animal that he surely was retirement hardly affected his daily schedule at all: he would continue to visit clients and at times accompany me to cast his expert eye over any difficulties that inevitably arose in the varied life of a London builder. Considering how much of his work was really just time spent socialising it was not surprising that his retirement came so easily, but with the passing of time which was inevitably accompanied by the passing of many of his long-term clients as well as close friends, he found himself more and more at a loose end, and so one day he made the decision to return to work. This time his work would not be in his old profession as a decorator but something quite different, as he went off daily with two of his daughters, my sisters Pauline and Karen, to join a third sister at her cafe, Carols Place in East Sheen. Cyril did washing up, table clearing and delivered the meals, all of course with his usual chatty humour, and regularly berated any customer that did not manage to clear his plate of food - which he never failed to remind them had been lovingly cooked by his daughter. It was perfect for Cyril, for he not only had the company of his three girls but also an almost endless supply of people with whom he could socialise, but more importantly, being the great character that he surely was, that he could entertain. He was the life and soul of the place, and boy did they all love him.

CHAPTER FIFTEEN

NICE ONE CYRIL

The Boers have got my daddy
My soldier Dad;
I don't want to hear my Mummy sigh,
I don't want to see my Mummy cry;
So I'm going in a big ship
Across the ocean waves,
And I'm going to fight the Boers, I am,
And bring my Daddy home again!
-Mills and Castling.

This was a song which was often performed by my father Cyril just as it had been by his own father as a small boy. Cyril loved to perform and so would march around with his arms swinging and belt it out with great gusto.

It is said that you should be careful for what you wish as it may come true, and such was to be the case for me in this particular instance.

With the death of Diana Princess of Wales on the last day of August 1997, the stage was set for what was to become the most intense and memorable September of my life.

Having left London in 1990 I now lived in a remote cottage on the edge of the Denbigh moors in North Wales, and remember well hearing on the early morning radio the news of the tragic death of this young and vibrant woman. My initial reaction to this sad news was something I still consider to be a strong possibility or, as I put it to my partner Judy, 'They've done her in.' I had long believed that her open taunting of those with whom she had failed so badly to connect could only lead to trouble, and so it seems it had. Like many other people in the world we watched the dramatic events unfold on the television. We were fascinated by the reaction of the huge amount of people of all ages, from all walks of life, from all countries, regardless of race or religion, which showed that there were so many people with whom she so clearly did connect.

As the days passed and the debates raged around the world, the people of Britain were stirred from their usual day-to-day slumber and were brought together in the most extraordinary outpouring of shared emotion, more usually reserved for the likes of great sporting events such as the Olympics or the World Cup. The gates of Buckingham Palace, and more especially Kensington Palace, which was to be Diana's final home in London, and a place in which I had worked during Cyril's successful career, were daily piled ever higher with more and more flowers, as people responded to her death and chose this as one way to participate in this enormous and historic event. At times such as these London really is at its very best, as people with a common cause seem to drop all their usual defences; this changes the whole feel of the usually fast-paced and anonymous city, and for the first time since I had left it some years before I found myself actually missing the Old Smoke, wishing that I was there to see the mountains of flowers, but also to participate as a Londoner in the special atmosphere of this time.

Sometimes wishes do come true, as I was to find out on the morning of Thursday the 11th of September. The weather was absolutely glorious and Britain was experiencing the always much hoped for, but seldom seen, Indian Summer, and when the telephone rang early on yet another hot and sunny morning, I had a strange feeling that something was wrong. The call was from my family in London, who informed me that Cyril had suffered a major heart attack, and was now on life-support in St. George's hospital in Tooting. I packed my bags and set off to the railway station, for what was to be my first train journey since the many that I had made as a boy with Cyril, so many years ago.

The four hour journey from Rhyl station in North Wales takes you through Chester on to Crewe and finally down the spine of England all the way to London. In a kind of altered state I found myself looking out at what was once one of Britain's finest possessions - our railway - and was shocked to see the run-down state of this once proud and vital service. Stations that I had last seen as a boy full of shining steam engines and carriages, teeming with the hustle and bustle of everyday life, were now decrepit and decayed, with rubbish strewn everywhere. It made me very sad to see how badly we had allowed this system to decline. The hours passed slowly, and I found myself drifting in and out of the past, remembering the many times I had been on train journeys with Cyril, following our football team, Chelsea, all over the country. The ghosts of the past literally surrounded me, with faces that I had not seen for many years coming and going, all, of course, hovering around Cyril, whose presence I could actually feel with me.

My mind went back to events that I thought were long forgotten, like the day when Cyril took me to see the Flying Scotsman, one of the greatest steam engines of all time. I would have been around four or five at the time, and, like all children, I was fascinated by these wonderful, almost living creatures. As we approached the plate where the driver stood dressed in his heavy work clothes, cap and all, he suddenly leant out and called down, 'Would you like to blow the whistle son?', Cyril didn't wait for my answer for he lifted me up into the driver's huge, rough hands, and he in turn lifted me to pull the cord. The noise was both terrifying and wonderful and it reverberated all around the wonderful old station. What a treat.

As the train approached London I could feel the energy of my old home increase with every mile travelled, and slowly I began the process of preparing myself for the maelstrom of family life in the very difficult and intense period to come, wondering all the time what news of Cyril awaited me at my destination. Arriving at Euston I was met by my brother-in-law, Raymond, who told me that Cyril's condition had not changed and he was still unconscious. So, things did not look too good.

We set off across London, and on the way passed both Buckingham and Kensington Palaces on this, the final day, before the huge array of flowers left by Diana's adoring public were to be removed. It was an incredible sight, but one which I could not help but feel carried a portent of things to come for myself and my family in the not too distant future. My wish had been granted, but I never dreamt that the price would be so high.

Something that had been on my mind was now explained, which was why Cyril was in a hospital across London, when he lived just a quarter of a mile from the expensively refurbished Chelsea and

Westminster, or St. Stephen's Hospital, as we all knew it. On the morning of his heart attack he had been attended by an ambulance crew, who of course knew him well (typical Cyril), but they had been unable to admit him to his local hospital, which was just five minutes away in his beloved Chelsea, because of ward closures. This had meant that he was to be taken on a twenty minute journey across London to St. George's in Tooting, which we were now approaching.

As expected, Cyril was not alone, for, as ever, the whole Devenport clan were awaiting me when I made my way up to the Intensive Care Ward where he lay: there were my four sisters, various brothers-in-laws, most of his grandchildren and his only remaining brother, Fred, all trying desperately to bring him back to us. Intensive Care Wards are incredibly sobering places, for not only are you faced with the sight of your loved-one lying there looking so helpless, connected up to all the monitors by tubes and wires, but you also have to share this space with complete strangers who are all in the same boat. The atmosphere is so thick that it's almost possible to sense the various spirits hovering around you, all caught in a kind of flux between this world and the next.

Our vigil was to last for the rest of the day and all through the long night ahead, the family taking it in turns to sit talking to Cyril, massaging his body, holding him, and trying just about everything we could to bring him back, but as the time passed it became clear that our job was not now to keep him here but to help him on his way upon his final journey. Having decided that it was time to release him we instructed the wonderful staff of the Intensive Care Unit, who had been so supportive and kind, to remove him from all the machinery that makes up the life-support system, and allow him to go on his way.

The whole family were now gathered all around Cyril, each of us holding a part of him, from his soft old feet to his kind and lovely face, his breathing slowed and finally stopped and he drifted away, surrounded by all those he loved most. It was the end of a wonderful life, and it would now be up to all of us to say goodbye to our dad in the best way we could, and try our best to send him off in a way that this popular and much-loved man deserved.

And so began the intense, and, as everyone knows, volatile period of planning the funeral, with all its requirements and decisions which, of course, have to be agreed upon in order to satisfy everyone involved with their own particular needs. Add to this the understandably high emotional state of everyone involved and it's quite amazing that things get done at all, but they do, as naturally they have to, and all one can hope is that you get it right first time, for that's all you've got - as in this instance there are no rehearsals. Cyril in life truly loved funerals, so much so that I would often joke with him that he was the only person I knew of with a season-ticket for the cemetery; but joking apart, funerals for Cyril ticked all the required boxes. They have the sense of occasion and respect which was so important to him, they are a social gathering - something which he truly enjoyed - and lastly, they usually involved a good booze-up - something that he was not likely to miss out on, except upon this one occasion.

Our first priority was to get Cyril home as soon as possible, but, having died on a Friday, no end of pleading from all of us could make it happen until Monday afternoon; so leaving the beleaguered undertakers to do their work we, as a family, set about the myriad things that have to be done in so short a space of time. Most of Saturday was spent on the telephone, slowly working through the long list of the many people that made up Cyril's life, not the most pleasant of jobs, but a necessary and ultimately rewarding one, for as you hear the familiar voices which reach across the years and come from all periods of your own life you get great strength from all of their support and kindness.

Having spent the weekend organising the funeral and attending to the many other things, such as preparing the best-room for Cyril's return home, I also found time in the evenings to wander around the streets of the Worlds End. Still in my kind of altered state, I walked the streets that I knew so well, that were once full of so many familiar faces and teeming with life. Sadly, this was no longer the case, for although the houses were now all occupied and ablaze with lights the streets were now eerily empty, only the occasional glimpse of our ghosts remaining, leaving their faint echoes of all the times past and all the fun that was had; the silence now so loud that it was almost deafening, and not a face, let alone a familiar face, to be seen anywhere.

   Monday was now upon us, and we were all eagerly awaiting the return of Cyril to his home for the last time where, as was family tradition, the best-room having been prepared, awaited him; but as will now become clear, Cyril, being the man that he was, had other plans. It had never been easy to manipulate a coffin up the narrow staircase of our house, and indeed, the undertaker had voiced grave reservations about the possibility this time, so upon their arrival I was summoned into the street to inspect Cyril's coffin. We stood together, with me scratching my head, gazing at the biggest coffin that had ever been to our house, for Cyril was over six feet tall. It was soon agreed that another place would have to be found for him, and that it could only be on the ground-floor. The ground-floor of number 17 was comprised of one long room - a sitting-room at the front with a dining area at the back end. This would have to do, as it was the only place possible for Cyril to be laid out. We all felt that Cyril had organised this himself, for having been at the centre of everything in life he wasn't about to change and miss out just because of a small thing like having died, so their he was placed, fittingly, having been a decorator, upon trestles right in the midst of us all, no longer the life, but most definitely still the soul, of the party.
   Dinner that first evening was something that I shall never forget. I was sat with my two sisters, Pauline and Karen along with their respective partners Raymond and Kevin at the table, and in his proper place at the head there lay Cyril in his coffin, surrounded by lilies. Swallowing was a little tricky that first night, so much so for my sister Karen's partner Kevin, that looking a little green in the gills he apologised and retreated from the table, quite understandably, unable to participate in this, which was, even for us Devenports, a most bizarre and original family ritual.
   It was great to have him back home in the house where he had spent the greater part of his life: the house where myself and my four sisters had all been born, and where he, along with our mother, had done such a great job of raising us all; we had been truly blessed to have had them both as our parents. During the few short days before he would leave us all for the last time, Cyril would be visited by

many friends and family, who came to pay their respects and say their goodbyes in the place where they had known him best, and as the days passed so did the covering of lilies increase, until he lay in a white fragrant bower. It was quite beautiful.

One afternoon I was sat talking to my mother's brother, Uncle Bill, who as you may recall had been more or less adopted, along with his brother Jim, by Cyril and my mother all those years ago. Now, Uncle Bill was a very gentle soul, a lovely man and someone of whom I can easily say there was not a bad bone in his body, so it was with more than a little trepidation that I opened the front door after seeing the large dark frame of one of the local characters pass our window. The character in question was my mate Eric Bingham, who had kind of adopted my parents as his own, always referring to them as Farver and Muvver. One day my mum, whilst standing at a bus stop with some friends in the busy Kings Road, was passed by Eric on his bike. Suddenly from across the road came the booming voice of Eric, 'Ello muvver'. Now it must be explained that Eric, though he had lived in England most of his life was, in fact, six foot plus of pure Jamaican muscle, so my mother was not too impressed by his claim to kinship - but she was amused, and it gave us all a good laugh. I opened the door and in strode Eric who, clutching his crutch, announced 'Hello Peter, just thought I'd bring the old chap to say goodbye to Farver'.

Uncle Bill's jaw dropped as he was confronted by the large black apparition that now stood in front of him, holding his private parts, or his three-piece-suite as he often referred to them. I introduced them, and Eric walked across the room to see Cyril. Now, Eric was rather proud of his physique and kept himself in great shape, and he and Cyril had their own personal banter, which usually revolved around the general size and well-being of their private-parts ... and I once found myself caught up in one of their games. At the time I lived just around the corner from Eric and so would see him quite regularly, and one Saturday night at one of my many parties, I came across them chucking back the beer laughing, fooling about and generally having a good time. Upon my arrival Cyril said to Eric, 'Here Eric, I've heard you've got a big one, let's have a look then'. Without hesitation Eric proceeded to uncoil his rather large appendage for all to see.

Cyril peered down and said, 'That's not a big one, my Peter's is bigger than that. Go on show him Pete!'

To say you couldn't see my heels for dust would be an understatement, for I fled from the room like I was being pursued by the hounds of hell. Nice one Cyril!

Having said his goodbyes to Cyril, Eric, with tears in his eyes, sat down with me and Uncle Bill to have a chat. In no time at all his tear-stained eyes were zooming in upon the bowl of fruit in front of him, and in typical Eric fashion he asked if he could have an apple. Well, I had been witness to Eric's insatiable appetite on many occasions, but this would be a baptism for Uncle Bill, something he had never seen before and would probably never see again. When Eric eats it is always with great energy and enthusiasm and so with his usual relish he set about devouring the biggest apple from the bowl, which was reduced to just the stalk in no more than three or four bites. Down it went, core, pips and all; there was never anything wasted when Eric was around. Pauline, my eldest sister, then appeared from the kitchen with cups of tea and a plate of biscuits; needless to say the same fate awaited the biscuits which, thankfully, Pauline had removed from the packet - for with Eric around you just never knew.

The funeral arrangements had reached a bit of an impasse, with three of my sisters wanting a simple affair with little fuss, but one sister, Sue, insisted upon the old-style funeral with the horse-drawn, glass-sided carriage, which was so favoured by the old London villains. After much heated debate we all thought that Sue had come around to our way of thinking; but we were in for a big surprise the next morning when I called in on the undertakers to finalise the arrangements. I was congratulated, much to my bemusement, on our choice of the traditional funeral, horses and all, and was then informed that Sue had been in shortly before to arrange this. Reaching home I informed the rest of my sisters of what Sue had been up to and, as would be expected, we were all furious with her - but this was all to no avail, for her mind was made up and she even insisted that she would pay for the whole thing herself if she had to. She fought her corner so hard that inevitably we all had to give in. This was something of such importance to her that to do otherwise would have been damaging to all of us - and as was the case with another iron lady, this lady was not for turning.

Friday, the day of the funeral, was soon upon us, and yet again just as it had done now for a few weeks, the sun was beating down and we were set for yet another hot London day. Flowers arrived all morning; this had certainly been a week for them, and in no time at all they were piled along the pavement outside several houses: it was a wonderful display of affection which included a step-ladder with a pot of paint and brush on top, a beautiful life-sized black Labrador representing all our Tommys, and a massive pint of beer made entirely of amber and white chrysanthemums. Having spent the last few precious days with Cyril in our midst, and he having received his final visitors, the undertakers arrived to close the coffin. We all said our last goodbyes, and prepared ourselves for the final act. He was carried from the house by myself, his bother Fred, his grandson Adam and his son-in-law Peter, who are all big guys - but boy, was he a weight; it was almost as if he didn't want to go. But we eventually managed to roll him into the back of the hearse and close the door for his final journey.

Above him was placed a beautiful white cross and along his side was placed a wreath bearing the name by which he was affectionately known by so many people – 'FARVE'. His flowers were so many that the undertakers could not manage them all, so the rest were taken in the cars of friends and family. The decision eventually reached by us to take Cyril on his last journey by horse-drawn carriage was now fully justified. The beautiful black horses with feather plumes drew the carriage up the street, proceeded by the funeral director in his top hat and tails, the hat respectfully removed, to lead us out into the busy Kings Road. We first turned left, away from the crematorium, to take Cyril on the journey which he had made more than any other - through the old Worlds End, passing the pubs that he knew and was known in, where people were gathered outside to pay their last respects. Upon reaching the Chelsea Conservative Club, where so many years before Cyril had become its youngest Chairman, his friends emptied their glasses onto the road in the direction in which he was travelling. It was all very moving.

The whole procession now turned and made its way back along the

Kings Road, passing Slaidburn Street one last time, to begin the six mile journey across London to Roehampton. Being Friday afternoon the traffic was quite heavy, and would not be helped by the gentle pace of the horse-drawn carriage with its accompanying snake of cars which was following Cyril as he passed many more of the pubs that he had frequented over the years.

While passing one such, the Duke of Cumberland in Fulham, which had been another of Cyril's favourite haunts, the most extraordinary and special thing occurred. In the car, along with myself and my four sisters, were my Aunt Dolly and the latest addition to our clan, my six month old nephew, Sam. Now Sam, like all babies, had been adored by Cyril, and just like all of us before him would be placed in the 'hole' as he called it, which was created by the seated Cyril's crossed legs, to be sung to as he was being jigged up and down. This was something that they both enjoyed enormously. Sam up until this moment had yet to speak his first words, so you can imagine our reaction as we passed the old London pub to hear him belt out as clear as day, the word 'Grandad!' We were all understandably gob-smacked, and in unison turned our heads away from the pub to stare at the little chap who was still looking over towards the Duke of Cumberland. Extraordinarily, he had not only chosen this difficult word as his first but had, it seems, also chosen such an appropriate place to say it. Who knows, maybe Cyril had waved a final farewell to the little boy who was to be his last grandson.

With the poor old horses now well and truly lathered due to the heat we continued on our way. People stopped and stared, with many bowing their heads as we passed at our gentle pace; this really made the whole journey just that bit more special, and all thanks to Sue who had been right all along, for this really was exactly what Cyril deserved. Thank you sister.

Cyril was, as I have stated many times, an absolute stickler for punctuality and considered it bad form to be late for anything - but there was one exception to his rule. He had always said, 'The only thing that I will ever be late for will be my own funeral.' - and boy, was he right. We eventually arrived at Putney Vale Crematorium for the 4 p.m. service at 4.30 p.m. - his prophesy fulfilled. Fortunately,

Cyril's was the last service of the day so no inconvenience had been caused. Even in death his considerate nature was still shining through.

As the procession came to a halt we were amazed to see the amount of people gathered there; the Chapel was filled to the rafters which required many people having to stand outside. It was a gathering of the many and varied elements of Cyril's life, being a collection of all kinds of people from all kinds of backgrounds: family, friends, ex-workmen, clients, and even a few people who had, as they told me later, 'stayed after the previous funeral because they knew something interesting was going on.'

They had all been touched by the special nature of this gentle giant who, just like a chameleon, had with the greatest of ease blended into all of life's many variations, putting everyone - from children to the elderly, from the boys down the pub to the aristocracy, completely at ease, for he had one of life's greatest gifts ... he was never anything other than himself. It was all very moving, and before we knew it The Beatles were belting out 'All My Loving', with which we chose to close the service. This song was a great favourite of Cyril's, and was sung by him to all of us over many years. It was a fitting finale and certainly true to all that knew him for he only ever gave his all and was never one to do anything by half.

With the service now over we all gathered outside the crematorium to stand in the warm sunshine, to talk with and thank the many people who had gathered there to pay their last respects. Cyril would have been in his element. With this part of what was such a special day now more than successfully completed, we made our way back to the Worlds End for the next stage in the proceedings - the stage that was certainly one of Cyril's favourites – a good booze-up. Many people returned with us to Slaidburn Street for what was, I believe, to be the last real gathering out on the street of old Worlds Enders. The old street was once again filled with life, as it used to be so many years ago: a time before it had become the deserted, over-priced and glorified car park which it remains to this day. The sound of children playing filled the air, the voices of the adults growing ever louder as the booze began to take effect, loosening our tongues and creating once again the atmosphere of a tight and vibrant community which now rang all around the old familiar houses, as we generally reminisced, sharing memories of things long past, the people we had known here, and some of the things that had happened over the years. The many street-parties, the joy of the many bonfire-nights with all their noise, colour, and, of course, danger, and the faces of so many characters were summoned back, their ghosts spinning all around us as their stories were told. It was very special.

    Times such as these are most precious, for I truly believe that upon the death of a loved one that a crack forms between this world and the next, which opens for just a short period of time, allowing one, if you should so wish, to look and listen to the passing shadows and barely audible whispers of all those times past. Such was the atmosphere on this special night, and you could literally feel Cyril's presence along with all his old chums that he had now joined in the next world, but who were all keeping a watching brief over us all until 2.a.m. when our day, but more importantly *his* day, was finally done. Bless you Dad.

Postscript.

It's said that 'when it rains it pours', and this was never more true for me than during this extraordinary September, as, in a fashion so typical of Cyril, he had timed his big event to be at the centre of two others.

It all began with the mountains of flowers given to Lady Di, and was soon followed by evermore flowers that were to surround Cyril for his final few days with us; and then there were all the people.

Living then, as I still do today in a remote cottage in North Wales, one does not tend to see too many people; lots of sheep for sure, but people are rare, so one would naturally assume that returning there after such a hectic and people-filled week in London things would quieten down. Not this time, however. September had not quite finished with me yet, for my return on Saturday was to be the first day of what would turn out to be a seven day party, being held to celebrate the fiftieth birthday of my partner Judy - something that I was not sure I really needed, for I was understandably exhausted.

I approached the house with great trepidation, having been driven home by my old friend Ronny, to be welcomed back, not only by Judy, but also the twenty or so friends who had so far arrived. Almost immediately all of my fears disappeared as I realised that after such a week as I had just had the only answer, just as with a hangover, was the tried and tested antidote used so often by Cyril, known as 'the hair of the dog'. So the cure for having been around lots of people was obviously - lots more people.

It turned out to be the perfect way to close this intense and sad, but overwhelmingly wonderful period of my life, and as the glorious weather continued to find myself surrounded by good friends, having fun - in fact, ... all very Cyril

Printed in Great Britain
by Amazon.co.uk, Ltd.,
Marston Gate.